Upton
and the
Army

Upton and the Army

Stephen E. Ambrose

Louisiana State University Press
Baton Rouge

Published by Louisiana State University Press
Copyright © 1964, 1992 by Stephen E. Ambrose
Manufactured in the United States of America
All rights reserved
Designed by Gary G. Gore

Library of Congress Cataloging Card Number: 64-21590
ISBN 978-0-8071-1850-4 (pbk.)

Published with the assistance of a Ford Foundation grant

The paper in this book meets the guidelines for permanence and durability of the
Committee on Production Guidelines for Book Longevity of the Council on
Library Resources. ∞

Louisiana Paperback Edition, 1993

To Judy

Introduction

In 1861 Emory Upton graduated from the United States Military Academy at West Point, New York. He went directly into the Civil War. Like many other regular army officers, his war experience was an unhappy one. Upton felt that, because of public hostility to professional soldiers, he did not attain the position he deserved. He reasoned that his personal failure resulted from a larger problem—the refusal of the American people to accept the regular army as the chief source of the nation's defense.

After the Civil War Upton did two things to strengthen the position of the regular army. First, he tried to make the public accept a definition of the army's role which would give it a monopoly on armed force within the United States. To show the need, he tried to convince the American people that the militia and volunteer systems had never provided an adequate defense. Then, to make the army capable of meeting its new responsibilities, he attempted to reform it.

Upton did not look to the American past for guidelines. Instead, he turned to the army admired by professional soldiers throughout the Western world—the Prussian army. Like his fellow professionals, Upton saw the victor in the Franco-Prussian War, not the citizen army that won the American Civil War, as the model to copy. Upton tried to translate Prussian ideas into American practice. He was not successful. His inability to understand the interrelationship between politics and war in a democratic state prevented him from fashioning an acceptable system. Still, later Army leaders did espouse his program and therefore it had an influence on the growth of the American army. Upton's contributions to American military policy were essential to the development of a modern armed force in the United States.

I have been extremely fortunate in the help and encouragement I have received in the process of completing this study. The late Professor William B. Hesseltine of the University of Wisconsin gave generously of his time and great knowledge. President Jim Dan Hill of Wisconsin State College, Superior, provided me with insights and information. Professors Russell Weigley of Temple University and Theodore Ropp of Duke University supplied me with ideas and criticism. Professor T. Harry Williams, Louisiana State University, Dr. James I. Robertson, Jr., of the Civil War Centennial Commission, Dr. Robert Dykstra, of *Civil War History*, Professors Edward Coffman and Chester Easum of the University of Wisconsin, and Professor Richard C. Brown, the State University, Buffalo, New York, all contributed to the manuscript. Research was greatly facilitated by the assistance of Colonel Vincent J. Esposito, United States Military Academy, Captain Victor Gondos, Jr., of the National Archives, Colonel R. H. Wiltamuth, Office of the Chief of Military History, Department of the Army, Mr. Werner F. Samuelson, of Appleton-Century-Crofts, Inc., Miss Charlotte Mary Read, Genessee, New York, County Historian, and Donald M. Love, Oberlin College. A special word of thanks is due Colonels John Elting and William Wade of the United States Military Academy. The staffs of the libraries of Louisiana State University, both in Baton Rouge and New Orleans, Tulane University, the State Historical Society of Wisconsin, the New

York Public Library, and the Library of Congress have all been helpful.

Peter S. Michie's biography of Emory Upton, published in 1885, has made my task easier. Michie sought to print as many of Upton's letters as possible, and he called on all of Upton's acquaintances for contributions. I have seen the manuscripts Michie used and have checked them against the printed versions. Michie made some selections, but no changes in wording. The result was an excellent volume. Whenever I quote Upton and the entire quotation is in Michie's book, I cite the book as it is more readily available; when I use more of the letter than Michie did, I cite the manuscript source.

I am deeply obligated to Dr. Richmond D. Williams and his staff at the Eleutherian Mills Historical Library, Wilmington, Delaware, for the exemplary manner in which they made their manuscript and printed materials available, and for the financial assistance from the library which made it possible for me to spend a summer working with materials in Wilmington.

S. E. A.

Contents

List of Illustrations

Upton and the Army

Youthful Reformer

He was the epitome of a professional soldier. Courageous to the point of recklessness, Emory Upton always went into battle at the head of his column. Devoted to his duty, he was honest and hard-working. Dedicated to his profession, he attempted to improve the American army's prestige and efficiency. Impatient with things as he found them, he tried to reform everything that he touched.

Upton was single-minded in his purpose. He never drank, smoked, or cursed, and seldom laughed. He was asocial to the point of being acutely uncomfortable in the presence of civilians. Except for a concern with religion, his interests were narrow. He read nothing outside his field. His ambition was great. "There was no enterprise too perilous for Upton," a friend said of him, "if only he might hope to gain credit or promotion thereby." [1] As a young man his rise was so rapid and constant that he became convinced that nothing was beyond him. He aimed to become America's most renowned soldier. When, at forty years of age, this goal seemed unattainable, he considered his entire life a failure and became mentally ill.

Yet Upton's achievements were great. He had an important influence upon the development of the military policy of the United States. He performed the essential task of transporting European military ideas and techniques to the United States and presenting them in a coherent, understandable form. Although he was never an original or a brilliant thinker, he was a painstaking worker. A prolific writer, Upton was a polemicist rather than a scholar, but he was a good one. Most American military reformers of the twentieth century have drawn upon his ideas.

Born on August 27, 1839, on a farm near Batavia, in the northwestern corner of New York State, Emory Upton was the tenth child and sixth son of Daniel and Electra Upton. The family traced its ancestry to John Upton, a Scottish Puritan who settled in Salem, Massachusetts, in 1650 and four years later married Eleanor Stuart. Early in the nineteenth century their son, Daniel, purchased a farm near Batavia, where, on September 30, 1821, he married Electra Randall. The Upton family had moved away from Puritanism to the Methodist church, and Daniel and Electra were zealous in their faith. They embraced the reform movements which swept upper New York State in the first half of the nineteenth century, concentrating on temperance and abolitionism.

Emory grew up on the edge of the "Burned-over District," an area so named because of the religious revivals and Pentecostal beliefs prevalent there. While Emory was a youth, Dorothea L. Dix toured the region to advocate kinder, more intelligent treatment of the insane. William Miller, of Hampton, New York, convinced thousands in the area that the Second Coming of Christ would take place on October 22, 1843. The Millerites sold all their goods and, to be closer to heaven, awaited the Second Coming on roofs, hilltops, and haystacks. Mother Ann Lee and Jemima Wilkinson of New York State founded "Universal Friend" communities on the basis of celibacy. John H. Noyes sought perfection and catharsis in sexual indulgence at Oneida, New York.

When Emory was nine years old, Elizabeth C. Stanton and Lucretia Mott launched at Seneca Falls a woman suffrage movement. That same year, 1848, the Fox sisters' spirit rappings and table turnings induced an outpouring of spiritualism. And above all, abolitionism captured the imagination of the people of the Burned-over District.

As a child, Emory imbibed reform. His parents taught him to love and respect God, to do his duty, and to try always to improve the world, but they also imposed a stern discipline upon Emory and punished him for many of childhood's innocent pursuits. In a world so badly in need of light, there was no time for foolishness.* By the time he reached his teens, Emory's brothers were making their contributions to society. His parents pointed out to him their achievements while urging him to emulate them. In the early fifties Daniel, a pillar of the local church, talked with Charles Grandison Finney, the famous revivalist and president of Oberlin College, and acquired scholarships for two of his sons, John and James, the oldest boys; they both graduated from Oberlin in 1853. John then began law practice in Michigan while James went out to win a reputation for himself as a militant free-soiler in Kansas. Both soon became important figures in their local Republican parties.

Goaded by his parents, Emory was determined to surpass all his brothers and do so in a field which none of them had usurped. As a fourteen-year-old he read a life of Napoleon and decided to be a soldier. The next time the local Congressman, Benjamin Pringle, called on the Uptons, Emory informed him of his ambition and asked for an appointment to West Point. Pringle was sympathetic, but urged the teenager first to acquire more education.[2]

---

* On his fortieth birthday, Emory forgave his father for the "many times he took advantage of my weakness to chastise me for acts which to a juvenile mind appeared perfectly proper." Peter S. Michie, *The Life and Letters of Emory Upton* (New York, 1885), 476–77.

His father was not a rich man, but Daniel Upton respected education and wanted his children to get as much of it as possible. In 1854 he garnered two more scholarships from Finney and sent his nineteen-year-old son Henry and fifteen-year-old Emory off to Oberlin. This was Emory's first trip from home.

The college community that Emory entered represented to him the outside world and reinforced the views his parents had inculcated in him. Oberlin, Ohio, had its origins in the early 1830's as a utopian community dedicated to creating an institution of higher learning for Christians. In the mid-thirties, following a great debate on slavery at Lane Seminary, Cincinnati, the abolitionist students at Lane left and transferred to Oberlin. They brought with them money donated by the New York merchant-reformers, Lewis and Arthur Tappan. Soon afterwards Finney became president of Oberlin.

The college was both coeducational and integrated— about 5 per cent of the student body was Negro—and served primarily as a training ground for evangelical preachers and abolitionists. The faculty emphasized personal responsibility and immediate duty to God, which was one reason Daniel sent his sons there; Oberlin served *in loco parentis*. Emory's father also approved of the school because the discipline was strict and the students, through Oberlin's manual labor systems, could pay most of their own expenses. Further, Oberlin emphasized religion. Students had to attend church and numerous revivals. At Oberlin, Emory learned that the world was in darkness, and that those who had seen the truth were under the solemn and pressing obligation to send abroad the light. He accepted and retained this as a guiding principle of his life.[3]

Since Henry and Emory's scholarships paid only their tuition, the boys had to work for their room and board. They got afternoon jobs at a local sash factory at eight cents an hour. They went to class in the mornings and studied at night and before breakfast, rising before 5 A.M. Emory's only respite from work came on Sunday afternoons when he retired into the woods around Oberlin. Even then he did not relax; he never forgot that he was at Oberlin in order to prepare himself for West Point, and in the woods he read military history.

When Emory and Henry decided to go home for Christmas vacation, they stocked up on crackers and cheese, found work on a lake steamer going from Cleveland to Buffalo, and made it home in time for the holiday. They returned to Oberlin in the same manner. After one of their Spartan repasts Emory remarked: "Say, Hen, if we ever become big men we will remember this as something funny." [4]

Emory spent only two sessions at Oberlin. He wanted to take from the college a solid groundwork in mathematics as a preparation for West Point, but Oberlin emphasized the liberal rather than the practical arts. Emory disliked poetry and music and found the classics tedious; still he did satisfactory work. Although he had a good command of the English language, he was a hesitant speaker and did poorly in his recitations. He rationalized his shortcoming by saying it was not essential to his goal; soldiers did not need to be orators, and if they ever had to make a speech, it would be in the face of the enemy, when orations were necessarily short. He thought he could handle that. Classmates later remembered that Emory was thin and wiry, heavily freckled with hair that stood almost straight up, and that he was always in a hurry, often cutting a person off in the middle of a remark to make his own observation. Emory never forgot his ambitions. Once, when a classmate was joshing him about his desire to be a great soldier, Emory flared up and forced the student to accept a bet. If Emory became a general before he was forty-five, the classmate would present him with an engraved revolver; if he did not, Emory would give the student books of corresponding value.

To prepare himself for the Academy, Emory slept without a pillow, to avoid becoming round-shouldered, and refused to crack a nut with his teeth for fear of harming them and failing the physical examination.[5]

In early 1856 Pringle awarded Emory the West Point appointment, and from then until June Emory spent every available hour studying in preparation for the entrance examinations. In June 1856, he went to West Point. Although one-quarter of the appointees failed either the physical or mental tests, he was successful in both and entered his first summer encampment.[6]

Emory found West Point a well-established school with a deserved reputation for quality. Founded in 1802 on the banks of the Hudson River in southern New York, the United States Military Academy was originally designed to give a modicum of engineering knowledge to army officers. But it had no consistent approach, no academic program, and no prestige. Then, in 1817, Sylvanus Thayer began his sixteen-year tour of duty as Superintendent. Thayer made the Academy one of the finest institutions of higher learning in the country and probably the best school for training potential officers in the world. Emory found that Thayer had converted West Point into an academic school. His curriculum was heavily scientific, with an emphasis on mathematics and engineering, but he also took courses in ethics, English, history, and two foreign languages, French and Spanish. He attended classes in small sections of less than twenty students, and made daily recitations. At the end of each semester, in January and June, he answered questions in an oral examination before the faculty and the Board of Visitors, a group of Congressmen, educators, and professional men invited by Thayer to the Academy in an attempt to make it popular. In his first experience as a soldier, Emory found himself placed in a company as a part of the Corps of Cadets. His officers were older cadets of the First, or senior, and Second, or junior, classes. After his first examination, he went into summer encampment with the Corps of Cadets, where he learned the rudiments of a soldier's life.

The sixteen-year-old Emory was delighted with West Point. The school attacked none of his basic beliefs, maintained a strict discipline that was familiar and therefore comfortable to him, and promised to give him the training he felt he would need to improve the world. It encouraged his ambition—cadets were ranked in a general standing each week, month, semester, and year—and frowned upon frivolous behavior. In the encampment, he rose at five o'clock in the morning, policed the grounds until five-thirty, drilled until six-thirty, prepared for inspection, ate breakfast at seven, went to parade at eight, artillery drill at nine, policed again, ate dinner at one o'clock, attended dancing class from three to four, policed again, went to infantry drill at five-thirty, evening parade and inspection at seven, supper at eight, and bed at nine-thirty.[7] Emory had learned from his parents that discipline and orderliness were virtues, and the emphasis placed upon them at West Point provided his life with the regimentation his upbringing required.

In September, after the completion of his first encampment, Emory moved into the cadet barracks and began his scholastic studies. His life in barracks during regular session was as regulated as it had been in the summer encampment. He rose at five-thirty, studied from six to seven, attended classes until dinnertime at one o'clock, studied from two to four, then read in the library—Plutarch and Caesar were his favorites—wrote letters until supper at six, and studied from seven to nine-thirty and taps.[8]

The organization of West Point gave Emory a sense of progress. He remained on probation until after an oral exam

in January, 1857, which he passed with marks among the
highest in his class. He then received his official appointment, or warrant, as a cadet. In June he passed another oral
examination, and went into his second summer encampment
ranking twenty-third out of fifty-nine in his class. Following
another successful academic year, in which he moved up to
seventeenth place, Emory had his only furlough—two
months in Batavia. While he was at the Academy, Congress
was experimenting with a five-year-course in place of the
old four-year-course, so following his furlough Emory still
had three years of study ahead of him.[9]

Life at the Academy soon became routine, but occasional
special events provided some variety. In September, 1856,
General-in-chief Winfield Scott visited the Academy and
reviewed the Corps of Cadets. The cadets reviewed Scott
more than he did them, for "Old Fuss and Feathers" appeared in a hat topped with an immense white cockade from
which rose a two-foot plume of yellow ribbon and feathers.
A fancy sword belt surrounded his large midsection, and his
dark blue pantaloons had a gold stripe two or three inches
wide. Upton and the other cadets discussed the outfit for
weeks.[10] During Upton's Second Class year the Prince of
Wales came to West Point and reviewed the cadets. The
Prince and his suite were mounted and, preceded by a pla-
toon of dragoons serving as escort, passed the line of cadets
at a gallop. "I have never experienced such queer feelings
before," Upton confessed, "and, had I not been under military discipline, I believe my enthusiasm would have given
vent to itself in cheers." After the review the officers of
the class were introduced to the prince. Upton, the Assistant
Instructor of Artillery, bragged, "I can now say that my
rustic hand has grasped the hand of royalty." [11]

Young and impressionable, Emory found the soldier's life
irresistible. The pomp and pageantry, the order, the sense
of purpose, the feeling of belonging to an organization of

men dedicated to a patriotic duty, appealed to him. In February, 1857, he told his younger sister Maria, "I am passionately attached to West Point, and would not give up my appointment here for a million dollars." [12] West Point instilled into Emory a sentiment of aloofness from and superiority to civilians; it taught him to take great pride in the achievements of Academy graduates and of the regular army. Emory extended this into a feeling of contempt for civilian soldiers, a feeling which most West Pointers of the time shared. Emory's views were strengthened in his Second Class course in tactics by *The Elements of Military Art and Science,* written by a former instructor at the Point who had graduated in the class of 1839, Henry Wager Halleck. The book was in large part an attack on the militia and a defense of the professional soldier. Halleck believed that only the professional had the requisite skill—and, he implied, moral qualities—to take command of the nation's armed forces in time of war. [13]

Influenced by Halleck's views, Emory and his fellow cadets were indignant at the practice of filling vacancies in the army with civilian appointments just before graduation day at West Point. The Secretary of War made the appointments to satisfy political friends of the administration. The result was that Academy graduates found themselves ranked, because of their later appointment date, by the civilians. [14]

In June, 1860, as he prepared for his examinations in drawing, ethics, chemistry, and tactics, Emory paused to reflect upon his four years of "constant confinement and regular duties" at West Point. He was satisfied with his general standing, which was now in the top ten, and looked forward to the time when he would graduate "and the key which is to unlock the honors and emoluments of our profession will be delivered into our hands." He declared that one of the major factors in his success at West Point had been the discipline given him by his parents. They were, he admitted, rigid, but their chastisement was given in love rather than anger and it had prepared him well. Emory's religious interests, first emphasized by his parents and later reinforced at Oberlin, remained with him. "The army," he complained, "is a hard place to practice religion; though few scoff at it, yet a great majority totally disregard it." He comforted himself with the thought that Christians had never disgraced the profession of arms. "On the contrary, they are those who have most ennobled it." He assured his family he would continue to seek the Lord. The reform impulse was still strong; in 1860 he declared that the causes of the troubled times were Mormonism, spiritualism, intemperance, corruption in politics, and above all slavery.[15]

Throughout his West Point career Emory suffered some social ostracism because of his views. In his first encampment, in reply to questions from southern classmates, Emory announced that he was an abolitionist. He was the first cadet who ever had the temerity to do so. From then on he was either snubbed by or forced to fight with southern cadets. The tension, itself a minute reflection of the national situation, reached a climax following John Brown's raid on Harpers Ferry. Wade Hampton Gibbes of South Carolina made some offensive remarks about Emory's supposed intimate association with Negroes at Oberlin. Emory demanded an explanation, Gibbes refused to give one, and the two arranged to fight with swords that night. A large crowd gathered on the first floor of the cadet barracks while Emory and Gibbes went upstairs into a darkened room. While the sentinel, a Fourth Class cadet, called for the corporal of the guard and the cadets cheered for their favorite, Emory and Gibbes fought. Soon they staggered down the stairs, Emory with a slight cut on his face. No one taunted him again.[16]

As civil war threatened, Emory began to consider the possibilities a conflict would open to him. "Our profession differs from all others," he believed. "It is a profession of fate and a fatal profession. A long war would make many of us, and prove the grave of as many." After Abraham Lincoln's election he proclaimed: "If the worst is to come and war follow, *I am ready.*" His motto would be "*Dieu et mon droit.*" He was thankful for his military education and promised to do his "full duty to God and my country." [17] During the secession winter, Upton sent long letters to his brothers and sisters. He proclaimed his love for the Union, his determination to fight for it, and his personal feelings of tremendous excitement. The great evil, slavery, for which southerners alone were responsible, must be abolished, by force if necessary. "Think of a slave republic in the nineteenth century!" he cried. Even the ignorant people of Italy were fighting for liberty while the "chivalrous" South fought for slavery. "As for myself," he continued, "I am ambitious, and desire fame, but I will stand by the right; for what is the worth of fame when purchased by dishonor?" [18]

As a potential professional soldier, Upton undertook in early April to analyze the possible course of the impending war for the benefit of his family. The South, he said, would be successful in one or two campaigns, because Confederate President Jefferson Davis was preparing for war, "while we are lying supinely on our backs." Davis was drawing all the talent he could from the army and was organizing and training his forces. The North's lack of preparedness was catastrophic, because every victory by the South "at the outset will require three defeats to offset." [19] In April, 1861, war began. The First Class cadets exchanged rumors that they would graduate early and go right into the army. Upton was enthusiastic about the prospect. He had no desire for the traditional furlough "when such exciting scenes are being daily enacted." There was a professional consideration— many existing vacancies in the army would be filled with civilian appointments if the class waited until June to graduate, whereas if it went into the Army in May high rank could be obtained in many regiments.* The system of cadet rankings had taught Upton and his classmates that they were expected to fight for higher rank, and they learned the lesson well. After hearing that the midshipmen at Annapolis were about to be graduated and sent on active duty, the First Class cadets at West Point prepared a petition to the Secretary of War asking for immediate graduation and assignment. Upton and twenty-nine others signed the petition; eighteen cadets, from the southern and border states, did not. "The Government will know who are loyal and who are traitors," Upton commented.[20] Congress responded favorably to the cadets' petition, and by May 4, the First Class had finished its examinations and was ready for assignment. Upton graduated eighth in a class of 45, so he could choose his arm, either infantry, cavalry, artillery, or the engineers. The engineers carried the greatest prestige, but offered the slowest advancement; the artillery promised fast promotion; the cavalry guaranteed excitement; the infantry would see the most action and thus offered the best opportunity for heroism.

There was a possibility of receiving a commission in the various state volunteer forces. The governors, who controlled

---

* A West Point graduate went into one of the permanent regular army regiments as the most junior officer in that regiment. If a particular regiment was short of officers, the graduate could count on rapid advancement—some even became first lieutenants immediately. Unfortunately for the cadets, the Secretary of War often gave commissions in the undermanned regiments to civilians just before commencement at West Point. Henry du Pont, also of the class of 1861, reflected Upton's feelings—and those of his classmates—when he told his parents, "They are filling up the vacancies in the Army with citizen appointments as usual, a great outrage to our class but nothing else can be expected from politicians." Du Pont to his mother, March 21, 1861, Henry A. du Pont Papers, in the Henry Francis du Pont Winterthur Manuscripts, Eleutherian Mills Historical Library, Wilmington, Delaware.

appointments, were short of experienced officers, and most were willing to give command of a regiment to a home state West Point graduate, with the volunteer rank of colonel. The men who received such commissions needed permission from the War Department; they kept their regular army rank while drawing the pay of the higher rank, and could return to their regular regiment whenever they pleased. In the volunteers they could expect rapid promotion, but they would serve under untrained generals and lead inexperienced men. Training at the Academy prejudiced West Pointers against civilian soldiers, and they needed strong inducements before taking up service with them.[21]

Upton decided to accept a position with the regular artillery. On May 6, 1861, the day of his graduation, he received a commission as second lieutenant in the Fifth United States Artillery. Eight days later, as the regiment filled to its authorized strength, he was promoted to first lieutenant. Meanwhile, the entire class had been ordered to Washington for temporary duty drilling volunteer regiments. Now twenty-one years old, Upton felt prepared for war. Relying on the twin pillars of his Christian convictions and his professional training, he expected either to die on the battlefield or to emerge from the conflict a hero. Filled with a self-confidence he was not yet mature enough to carry, Upton appeared to be insufferably pompous. But he was concerned neither with appearances nor opinions. The great crusade was under way, and he was going to be a part of it. He had an opportunity to both help reform the world and to satisfy his own ambitions and he impatiently awaited his first trial at arms.

The Civil War: The Climb

Displaying courage, ambition, opportunism, and intelligence, Emory Upton emerged from the Civil War as one of the outstanding young officers in the United States Army. During the course of the conflict he served with distinction in the artillery, infantry, and cavalry. He became a brevet major general and commanded a cavalry division. Upton was always willing to experiment in the field, and he made important contributions in practical tactics. After the war General James H. Wilson said of him, "He was a military enthusiast and student of extraordinary ability, courage, and judgment, and, young as he was, I have never doubted that when the war ended he was the best all-round soldier of his day." [1]

Upon graduation in May, 1861, Upton was assigned to the Fifth United States Artillery Regiment. After arrival in Washington he found himself loaned to the Twelfth New York volunteer regiment, under the command of Colonel Daniel Butterfield. He spent most of May drilling the volunteers, which he confessed was tiresome and difficult, but "I do not complain, when I think how much harder the poor privates have to work." [2]

Upton would later say that the army of which he was a

part "presented to the world the spectacle of a great nation nearly destitute of military force." The regular army numbered 16,367 officers and men, 90 per cent of whom were stationed on the frontier. The militia was "so destitute . . . of instruction and training that . . . they did not merit the name of a military force." Still, the President had to rely on it as his main source of strength. The regular army, designed to fight Indians and currently engaged in that task, was unprepared to prosecute a major war. It had no general staff to make plans; its bureaus were headed by old men who regarded their posts as sinecures; the General-in-chief was a septenarian who, for fear of doing irreparable damage to the regular army, resisted all attempts to scatter regular officers among the militia units, where they might have taught the men something of the military art; the ablest graduates of West Point had left the army for civilian life. Through reliance upon volunteering and conscription, the United States eventually created an excellent army, but it did so at immense cost. Upton was outraged at what he saw in the first days of the Civil War, and he never forgot it.[3]

In the spring of 1861, Upton feared that, while others fought the battles, he would have to spend the entire war teaching volunteers the rudiments of a soldier's life. When, on May 24, troops moved out of Washington into Virginia, Upton thought that the first—and perhaps only—great battle of the war would take place without him. He applied for a transfer and, on May 27, became aide-de-camp to Brigadier General Daniel Tyler of the First Division, Department of Northeastern Virginia. On June 1, he left for Virginia with General Tyler and in the next week went on several scouting missions. Once, finding some skirmishers poorly deployed by a political colonel of a Michigan regiment, Upton redeployed them and thereby won Tyler's approval.

On July 21, 1861, Upton's first real opportunity came.

Tyler's division moved around Centerville and as far as Blackburn's Ford on Bull Run, where Upton aimed and fired the opening gun of the battle. He then participated in a charge against the enemy across the creek. Although wounded in the left side and arm by a Minié ball, he remained on the field. In the latter stages of the battle, he crossed Bull Run above the Stone Bridge with the Sixty-ninth New York Infantry. Riding in front of the men, Upton stumbled upon a regiment of southerners. As both sides wore a great variety of uniforms, and one could never be sure, Upton asked if they were rebels. When they responded affirmatively, he tried to ride to the side so that the New Yorkers would have a clear field of fire, but he was too slow, and his horse was shot from under him. Removing the saddle, Upton proceed to a nearby house, where he found Owen Lovejoy, the noted abolitionist, tending to the casualties. Upton explained his position to Lovejoy and borrowed his horse. The rest of the day, although weak from loss of blood, Upton delivered messages from General Tyler. That night, the twenty-one-year-old officer described the battle: "I regret to say we are defeated. Our troops fought well, but were badly managed." [4]

In August, 1861, upon recovery from his wound, Upton was attached to Battery D, Second United States Artillery, in the defenses south of Washington. Despite his experience at Bull Run, Upton still expected the war to follow the set rules he had learned at West Point, and he was shocked at the conduct of the volunteers in Virginia. An undisciplined mob of barbarians, they "burned buildings, destroyed furniture, stole dishes, chairs, etc., killed chickens, pigs, calves, and everything they could eat." Still his abolitionist feelings remained—he denounced slavery as a moral, political, and social evil and hoped it would be destroyed forever. But he did not make the connection between the two views; he did not understand that the ideology he professed unleashed the forces of destruction he denounced. And later, as an advocate of army reform, he never saw that the nature of modern, ideological warfare necessitated the mass army and made obsolete the purely professional, disciplined army, fighting civilized war according to traditional rules. Upton's organizational abilities and tight discipline brought him to the attention of the higher echelons of the army. While reviewing troops in March, 1862, General Irwin McDowell asked, "Which is Upton's battery?" Pleased and encouraged by the recognition, Upton declared, "Give me one chance, and I shall be quite contented; and, if I don't acquit myself with honor, you will never see me again."

In late April, 1862, when his battery became a part of William Franklin's division, Upton moved to the Virginia Peninsula with George B. McClellan's army. On the morning of May 7, Upton arrived at West Point on the York River. A battle was in progress. Held in reserve until noon his battery finally took position in the center of a large field, about 1,400 yards from the enemy's firing position. Setting his fuses at five seconds, Upton opened fire, only to find that the fuses were unreliable and most of the shells were bursting short of the mark. Switching to solid shot, he drove the enemy from his works. "His accurate firing," Upton's commander reported, "contributed greatly to the repulse of the enemy, and gave all our troops on this flank increased confidence." [5] During the remainder of the Peninsular campaign Upton continued to display traits not only of a capable commander, but of an imaginative one. He earned promotion to command of an artillery brigade, consisting of four batteries of twenty-six guns, in the First Division, VI Corps. He distinguished himself in the Maryland campaign of 1862, especially at Crampton's Gap and at the battle of Antietam. In the latter engagement his accurate firing from near the center of the Union line (where once again he abandoned the unreliable shells for solid shot) drew favorable comment. "The artillery," he decided, "is a pretty arm, and makes a great deal of noise." He confessed that combat was pleasing: "From the time we left Alexandria till the close of the battle of Antietam, I never spent any hours more agreeably or enjoyed myself better."

Although he was happy making war, Upton was dissatisfied with service in the regular army. His West Point-trained superiors regarded him with esteem, and as a member of their small fraternity he could always count on preferential treatment from them, but the sphere in which the professional soldiers—even the major generals—could make their influence felt steadily diminished as the Civil War increasingly became a civilians' war. The great majority of regiments in the Union army were state volunteer forces, and the only path to rapid advancement lay with service in the volunteer units because only there could an officer command large bodies of troops and distinguish himself.

In October, Upton was ordered to West Point as an instructor. Seeking to avoid the assignment, he went to Washington where he heard that Colonel Richard Franchot of the One Hundred Twenty-first New York Volunteer Infantry had declared himself unfit for the military life, run successfully for Congress, and resigned his commission. Upton contacted New York State politicians and acquired the command—with a promotion to colonel of volunteers—of the One Hundred Twenty-first. Years later a friend, recalling the incident, remarked, "From the beginning Upton was ruled by an insatiable ambition to reach the heights of his profession." [6] Upton made a favorable impression upon his regiment. One soldier described him as a young-looking man with light mustache, high cheek bones, thin face, and a strong, square jaw. He had a small mouth and thin, usually tightly closed lips, which made his mouth look even smaller. His deep blue, deep-set eyes "seemed to be searching all the time." He had dark brown hair, a dark complexion, and an intensely serious look, emphasized by his moral rigidity—a well-worn Bible was always on his desk—and lack of humor.

Like most Civil War volunteer units, the One Hundred Twenty-first New York needed discipline. Upton moved it out of the wooded area in which it was camped into an open space where he could conduct daily drills and inspections. He began a series of severe tests, based upon West Point tactics, for the officers. To the great delight of the 657 men in the regiment, this resulted in several resignations by disgusted politicians. Upton then got the state authorities to agree never to appoint an officer to the One Hundred Twenty-first until he had been approved by Upton himself. Applying his knowledge of army administrative technique, Upton improved the quality and quantity of the food and clothing the men received. Soon after he began his campaign, the One Hundred Twenty-first was known as "Upton's regulars." It retained the name to the end of the war.[7]

In November, after Ambrose Burnside replaced George B. McClellan, Upton and his regulars moved with the Army of the Potomac across the Rappahannock River to Fredericksburg. In the ensuing battle, the One Hundred Twenty-first was on the left of Burnside's line. Since the hills in its front were too steep to justify an assault, the regiment spent most of the day engaged only in skirmishing. Burnside's disaster at Fredericksburg led to the elevation of Joseph Hooker to command of the army. In the spring of 1863, Hooker launched an attack on Robert E. Lee's army that consisted of a two-pronged thrust. The major part of the army moved west along the river with Hooker, then crossed and attempted to turn Lee's left. General John Sedgwick, with some 30,000 men including the One Hundred Twenty-first attacked the Confederate troops at Fredericksburg. Sedgwick hoped to pin them down while Hooker swung around the southern left flank.

Since Lee had pulled the majority of his men out of

Fredericksburg, Sedgwick gained control of the heights above the city with relative ease. He then turned west towards the main body of General James Longstreet's corps, which was between Sedgwick and Hooker's main body. Near Salem Church the One Hundred Twenty-first, on the left of Sedgwick's advancing line, ran into a belt of timber held by the Confederates. At five-thirty on the afternoon of May 3, Upton launched an attack. It promptly ran into heavy fire. Upton rode ahead to encourage his men, who gave a cheer and eagerly followed, but the Confederates were using smoothbores with three buckshot and a bullet to each charge, and their next volley cut the Union troops down in rows. Upton turned in his saddle and shouted to his men to fall back. It was an expensive lesson. The One Hundred Twenty-first went into the battle with 453 men; its losses were 104 killed and 174 wounded. Of every 100 men who charged, 61 were casualties. Never again did Upton attempt a frontal, daytime assault until careful preparations had been made. In his first infantry attack, Upton learned to appreciate and thus fear the power of nineteenth-century weaponry; in the postwar period one of his major contributions would be a new system of tactics (based on a strong skirmish line), an open order, and advance by rushes instead of direct linear assault.[8]

After Chancellorsville, the decimated One Hundred Twenty-first received reinforcements and Upton faced an insurrection. His new men were three-year volunteers from four New York regiments which had been disbanded when the majority, who had enlisted for one year, finished their service time. The volunteers had been promised that they would be retained in the same regiment or discharged with the rest, and they insisted that the government must keep its promise despite the need for them in the One Hundred Twenty-first. Upton appealed to their pride and patriotism— at the same time telling them that he was determined to keep them in the army and would enforce a rigid compliance with his orders. The reinforcements nevertheless lodged a formal protest, and a board of investigation reported in their favor. Secretary of War Edwin Stanton, however, dismissed the case. He contended that the men had enlisted for three years and the government could not be responsible for the illegal action of its agents or any false promises made by them. The new men had hardly been integrated when the regiment faced another challenge. Following the Confederate victory at Chancellorsville, Lee slipped away from Hooker and marched north. The Army of the Potomac followed, with the One Hundred Twenty-first in the rear. The regiment spent most of June marching in miserable weather. On the night of June 14, Upton's men moved to Fairfax Station, Virginia, in a driving rain and intense darkness that was relieved only by vivid flashes of lightning. The mud, stirred by the thousands who had preceded them, was deep and movement tedious. Then after two days of rest and hot sunshine, the New Yorkers again took the road, which had now turned to red-clay dust, causing a choking thirst among the men in the rear. On June 29, the regiment passed New Market. Urgency increased as it moved farther north towards the impending battle. Upton rode up and down the lines, urging the men to keep the lines tightly closed. He soon had the regiment making five miles an hour. Jests passed among the men, audible enough for the officers to hear, that the horses would soon play out and then the troops could rest; that night, just after the soldiers spread their blankets, orders came to pack up and move out. The men were once again on the road. This time there was no jesting.

On July 1, General J. J. Bartlett moved up to divisional command; he appointed Upton to replace him as commander of the Second Brigade, First Division, VI Corps. Determined to arrive at Gettysburg in time for the battle, Upton wore

his brigade to the point of exhaustion that day, covering
thirty-two miles. Many footsore men tried to drop out of the
ranks, but after Upton made examples of a few stragglers by
firing upon them the rest of the weary men resumed their
march. But all his efforts were wasted. Upon arrival at
Gettysburg, Upton received orders to occupy the left of Little
Round Top, the scene of intense fighting the day before but
now far removed from the heart of the conflict. Upton's men
suffered no casualties and never engaged the enemy—they
had to content themselves with cheering for the Union troops
who repulsed George E. Pickett's charge. The First Division
of the Corps did lead the pursuit of Lee, but despite a few
minor skirmishes it never became actively engaged. Upton
could find consolation only in his promotion. "The command of a brigade is a half-way step between colonel and
brigadier general," he said, "and I shall try to take the
full step in the next battle." [9]

In the post-Gettysburg maneuvering, Lee eventually
halted and established a strong position on the south bank
of the Rappahannock River. On November 7, the VI Corps,
leading the Army of the Potomac, arrived at the river and
found that Lee had a bridgehead on the north bank at Rappahannock Station. The bridgehead would enable Lee to
recross the river and strike at George Meade's flank when,
and if, feasible. The Confederates had a redoubt on a bluff
near an old Orange and Alexandria Railroad bridge and a
line of rifle pits extending up the river to give protection
to a newly laid pontoon bridge. General David A. Russell,
commanding the Third Brigade of the First Division, attacked and carried the redoubt, but had trouble holding it
because of enfilading fire from the rifle pits. At dusk he asked
Upton to bring up the Second Brigade. Upton led the men
at double time to the redoubt; the soldiers loaded muskets
as they moved forward. When Upton arrived, Russell asked
him to dislodge the Confederates from the rifle pits.

Darkness now covered the field. Upton left one regiment in reserve, then had the remainder of his men unsling their knapsacks and fix bayonets, gave them strict orders not to fire and to creep forward. When within thirty yards of the pits, Upton whispered orders to his men to charge silently. At the point of the bayonet, without firing a shot, the brigade drove the surprised Confederates from their works.

The enemy was routed and confused. Most of the Confederate troops were wandering around in the darkness between their old works and the bridge. Upton saw that he had an opportunity not only to cut off the Confederates on the north side of the river but also to capture the pontoon bridge intact. He ordered one of his two regiments to move down to the river and take up a position at the foot of the bridge. With the other regiment Upton made ready to attack. His final preparation was a short speech. In two sentences, Upton invoked home and country to inspire his men, and heaven to console them; in two more he extracted fear from his own troops and placed it in the enemy's: "Men, your friends at home and your country expect every man to do his duty on this occasion. Some of us have got to die, but remember you are going to heaven." Raising his voice to make sure the Rebels heard him, Upton continued, "When I give the command to charge move forward. If they fire upon you, I will move six lines of battle over you and bayonet every one of them."

Giving a yell, the men charged. The enemy, fearful of Upton's "superior force," tried to escape across the bridge, discovered that Upton already held it, and threw down their arms. The Confederates on the south bank then tried to burn the bridge, but heavy musketry from Upton's men stopped them. The bridgehead was gone.[10]

Meade failed to follow up Upton's victory at Rappahannock Station. The lethargy that engulfed the Army of the Potomac for the remainder of 1863 gave Upton an opportunity to meditate upon the course of the war. He agreed with Meade's policy of avoiding a battle, because he thought the North should build up an overwhelming force in the East before attacking. The vast distances involved in campaigns in the West made victories there fruitless. Therefore Ulysses S. Grant's army should be transported to the East, where it could help fight Lee's army. Upton did not expect his ideas to be adopted, but "perhaps I may be right; if so, of course it would strengthen my confidence in my judgment."

Upton also decided that the main cause for the North's failures was poor leadership. The young officer had a simple solution to the complex problem. He maintained that Americans made the best soldiers in the world—after they had been trained—but older commanders were incapable of calling forth their inherent qualities. By neglecting to make stirring speeches before a battle, getting out in front of the men and encouraging them during an engagement, and thanking them afterwards, the generals missed many opportunities. The implication was clear—younger men should be given more important commands.

For himself, Upton was determined to be a great leader. In November, he read Plutarch's *Lives* and declared, "I can not fail to see the charm success lends to military life. Victorious in every battle, courage rewarded in every struggle, who could not follow a Caesar or a Napoleon? Success begets confidence and resolution."

But his own successes had not been rewarded—he was still a colonel. At one point Meade told him that without "political influence" he would never be promoted. This prompted Upton to make a long denunciation of "paltry politicians." In April, 1864, he said, "I ought to have had it [a brigadier general's commission] a year ago." He added that he had left "abundant proof that I earned the honor, but it was unjustly withheld." Upton began to feel that a conspiracy had been formed to deprive him of his just rewards.

He determined to make one last effort, however. "I have not fully despaired of receiving promotion, but I have despaired of receiving it in the manner honorable to a soldier. It is now solely the reward of political influence, and not of merit, and this when a government is fighting for its own existence." [11]

In 1863, eight brigadier generals and seven major generals, headed by Meade, Hooker, Butterfield, and Sedgwick, recommended Upton for promotion. All bestowed the highest praise on him. Major General Robert Schenck said that Upton was "remarkable for his zeal, intelligence, and gallantry." Still the New York politicians ignored him.

In 1864, Upton tried it the politician's way. He wrote to New York Senator Edward D. Morgan about a vacant brigadier-generalship for New York. "I only ask that the recommendations of my superior officers may be compared with those of the other applicants," he said. Upton asked the officers in the Second Brigade to write Morgan, which they all did. A Cherry Valley, New York, resident, who had been visiting his two sons in the One Hundred Twenty-first New York, wrote a letter of recommendation to Morgan. Michigan officers bombarded their governor; so did one of Upton's brothers, a Michigan resident, and Governor Austin Blair wrote Lincoln in behalf of Upton.[12] But all Upton's efforts were fruitless. Despite his record Upton, with no significant political support, did not get a promotion and he never forgave the state governors for the slight. A decade and a half later he told an associate, "The fallacy of state sovergnity must be exposed. It is the root of all the weakness in our military system." [13]

In the spring of 1864, Grant became General-in-chief and personally directed the Army of the Potomac in what he hoped would be its last campaign against Lee. Upton commanded the Second Brigade of the First Division of the VI Corps. On May 4, 1864, his brigade crossed the Rapidan

River at Germanna Ford; by the next day, despite fires in the woods along the road set by the enemy to impede the advance, Upton had reached Wilderness Tavern. On May 7, he received orders to send reinforcements to the extreme right of the VI Corps, which the enemy had turned. He chose the One Hundred Twenty-first New York and the Ninety-fifth Pennsylvania. The men started off at double time only to encounter a strong enfilading fire from their left. Their line stretched out by the narrowness of the road and the quickness of the march, the men could not prevent large masses of the enemy breaking into their ranks and throwing them into confusion. Upton mounted his horse and rode out to the position. Using the flat of his sword, he rallied about half of the men, then charged through the woods and restored order. That afternoon Upton's men moved through Chancellorsville to Piney Branch Church, then down the Spotsylvania road until they came upon the V Corps engaged in a fire fight with the enemy. But as Upton prepared to aid his embattled friends, he was struck in the right flank. Changing front, he beat off the Rebel attack. The brigade then entrenched in its positions for the night.

In the first few days of the campaign neither Grant's strategy nor his tactics had been successful; as was usual in the Civil War, the side on the defensive had had much the better of it. If the side on the strategic offensive hoped to win the war, new ideas, new concepts, and a new system of tactics were needed.

Since the fifteenth century and the widespread introduction of the handgun, tactics had followed essentially the same pattern. Previously, generals had relied upon the weight of their charge to break an enemy line, and the greatest weight was attained through an attack in column. With the new weapon, however, generals realized they could bring more firepower to bear by spreading their men and making a linear charge, thus giving every soldier an opportunity to fire. Such tactics continued to dominate the nineteenth-century battlefield—Upton used them at Salem Church.

The fundamental problem involved in a linear attack was that the long, thin lines presented an easy target to the defenders. Before the introduction of the easily loaded rifle, this was unimportant, because the enemy could fire its smoothbored pieces only when the attackers were within fifty yards. In the American Civil War, however, because of the widespread use of the fast-loading rifled musket, which was longer-ranged and more accurate than the smoothbore, the old-fashioned linear attack was little short of murder. Generals on both sides suffered enormous casualties for no discernible gain at Malvern Hill, Fredericksburg, Gettysburg, Vicksburg, Cold Harbor, and elsewhere. The defensive infantry began firing at 500 yards or more range and usually got off eight or ten volleys in five minutes. This left the attackers decimated *and* short of their objective.[14]

In the Civil War, important tactical changes most often came from brigade or regimental commanders who were close to the fighting and knew at first hand the effect of the rifle and of entrenchments, which, by protecting the enemy, made it even easier for him to break an attack. For three years Upton had been mulling over the problems rifling presented to the offensive. He saw this as his first opportunity to make an important reform in this field of tactics where the army most needed improvement. Although unwilling to give up the firepower of the linear attack, still he felt that in certain circumstances (particularly when there was open ground between the two forces) it was more important to come to grips quickly with the enemy than to achieve maximum firepower. Upton began to advocate an attack in column, mounted from close to the enemy's works. The disadvantage was that most of the men could not fire, because of the pres-

ence of their friends in front of them, while they were exposed to a flanking fire. But the advantages were great. By
initiating their charge from close up the attackers reduced
the number of volleys they would receive, while the weight
of their column would force a breach in the enemy's lines,
which could be exploited in order to create flanks where
none had existed before. And the column would put enough
men in the enemy lines to enable the attackers to hold their
gains. Many other junior officers in both armies had suggested tactical changes since linear tactics were no longer
satisfactory, but Upton had two advantages—he had outlined a method of attack that was simple and traditional,
and he was in a position to try his idea at once. Grant and
Meade listened to it with interest, and promised to give
Upton an opportunity to test his method.[15]

By the afternoon of May 10 Upton's brigade was in position just to the left of Winfield S. Hancock and Gouverneur
K. Warren's corps. They had made a savage and costly assault that day. Upton's corps faced the southeast and a small
wooded area. A narrow road ran through the wood and
played out in a field which sloped up some 200 yards to the
enemy's works. In front of their trenches the Rebels had
cut trees, sharpened the branches, and pointed them towards
the Yankees. They covered the trench itself with a solid
wall of logs and banked-up earth, topped by a head log
which was blocked up a few inches above the dirt. This
gave the Confederate riflemen an opportunity to stand in
the trench, aim and fire through the slit, and enjoy almost
complete protection. They also had constructed heavy traverses—dirt mounds running back from the trenches at right
angles—to protect themselves from enfilade fire. One hundred yards to the rear the Rebels had another, unfinished
trench. The troops facing Upton occupied the left, or western, side of what would later be known as the "Bloody
Angle." It was not a tempting spot to attack—in that 200

yards of open space any linear assault would bog down, never even reaching the Confederate works. But Grant was eager to keep up the pressure on the Confederates, and Upton was anxious to try his method. Grant passed the necessary orders on to Russell, now division commander, who then selected twelve outstanding regiments and called Upton to him. Taking from his pocket the list of the regiments, he handed it to Upton and asked, "What do you think of that for a command?"

Upton replied, "I golly, that is a splendid command. They are the best men in the army."

Russell then told Upton that he was to use the men to experiment with an attack in column. Russell added, "If you do not carry [the enemy works] you are not expected to come back, but if you carry them I am authorized to say that you will get your stars."

"I will carry those works. If I don't I will not come back," Upton replied.

While Meade, Hancock, Warren, and Burnside stationed themselves on hills from which they could observe the attack, Upton prepared his column. Calling the regimental commanders to the front, he explained his plan of attack to them and placed the men in three lines, each four regiments deep. He instructed the leaders of the One Hundred Twenty-first New York, in the center of the front line, and of the Ninety-sixth Pennsylvania, on the right, to turn to their right as soon as they had gained the enemy works and to charge a Confederate battery there. The Fifth Maine, on the left of the front line, would change front to the left and open an enfilading fire upon the enemy. The men in the second line were to halt at the works and fire to their front, with the third line supporting them. The fourth line would advance to the edge of the woods, lie down, and be prepared to advance through the breach if all went well, or to meet a counterattack if it did not. By attacking, in effect, in waves,

the men would present less of a target. Upton emphasized
that he wanted all the regimental commanders to shout the
word "forward" constantly. To the men themselves the
young colonel gave explicit orders. Each was to have his
musket loaded and bayonet fixed, but only the men in the
three leading regiments were to cap their muskets. General
Gershom Mott's division, on Upton's left, would support the
charge.

Just before 6 P.M. a short artillery preparation began; ten
minutes later, when the bombardment ceased, Upton motioned his men forward. They crept to the edge of the wood.
Then, when Upton yelled "Forward!" the men sprang to
the charge. Ignoring a heavy front and flank fire, the first
two lines sped to the parapet, where a hand-to-hand conflict ensued. The Confederates, driven down into their pits,
sat with their loaded rifles held upright, bayonets fixed,
ready to impale the first Union head that appeared over the
top. After the leading men fell, Minié balls or bayonets
through their heads, some of the men in the next line held
their pieces at arm's length, pointed them over the parapet,
and fired straight down. Others grabbed their rifles by the
barrel and used the stocks as clubs, swinging them over
the topmost log. Some pitched their bayoneted rifles over
the parapet like harpooners spearing whales.

The struggle was furious but short. Upton's numbers pre-
vailed, and his men began jumping over the top into the
Rebel trench. As the first line turned to the right and left,
the second and third lines pressed forward and occupied the
enemy's second line of entrenchments. The fourth, or reserve line, excited by the success, came forward without
orders. Upton had proved his point. Attacking a strong position in the enemy line he had broken it and forced an
opening through which at least a division could have moved.

But the reinforcements were not ready. Worse, Mott's
division on Upton's left failed to make anything like a proper

supporting attack. Upton's men would say later that Mott was drunk. The enemy, regaining confidence, began to move reinforcements against Upton's front and flanks.

With all of his men committed, Upton was now three-fourths of a mile ahead of the main Union line, with no prospect of any support. When a Confederate battery began to enfilade his lines from the left, he pleaded for volunteers to rush it. None came forward. He called for men from the One Hundred Twenty-first New York, saying, "Are there none of my old regiment here?" Most of them were dead or wounded. Just then an order came from Russell to withdraw, and Upton gave up his hard-earned position. His losses were about 1,000 men killed and wounded, and he inflicted equal casualties on the enemy and captured 1,200 prisoners. Moreover, he had shown that if a charge were properly handled, closely mounted, and made in column rather than in line, a strong trench position could be carried. There were other lessons: charges by column had to be well supported on the flanks; surprise was important to the operation; reserves should be ready to exploit a breakthrough.[16]

Upon his return to the main line, Upton put his men in position and then went to see Russell at VI Corps headquarters. Depressed, he muttered about his own great losses and the lack of support. Finally he got up to go to his tent for the night, and as he was leaving, Russell told him to drop by in the morning. Russell hunted up a pair of stars, then went to the Corps Commander, General Horatio Wright, and said, "General, you remember when Colonel Upton was selected to lead the charge it was with the understanding that if he took the works he was to win his stars. Now I think he ought to have them." Wright concurred and telegraphed Meade, who responded "certainly," and wired Washington. Lincoln replied that night that he had drawn up and signed the commission.

General Russell made some comments about how much

Upton deserved his stars the next morning, then handed them over with, "Here they are." Upton took them in his hand, looked at them, then at Russell; he remarked how his men would be proud and happy to know that their efforts had been appreciated, opened his knife, and cut off his eagles. He found some thread, sewed on his stars, and rode to his men to show them off.

"I am disposed to think that it will be better in the end for me to have received my promotion at this late date," he decided later that day. "The reasons for [it] are gratifying to any soldier. It will be entered upon the records of the War Department that I was promoted for 'gallant' and distinguished services." [17] Two days later Grant, encouraged by Upton's success, decided to launch a heavier attack with his left. After some early gains, the attack bogged down. Upton moved his brigade forward to support it. Arriving at the point of the Confederate line, which was refused on both sides, Upton was engaged in the most sanguine conflict of the war—Bloody Angle. For eighteen hours his men fought the enemy. Neither side was really on the offensive or defensive; both were merely trying to hold what they had and kill as many of their opponents as possible. Upton noticed that a large red oak in his front furnished shelter to the Confederates from which they could fire upon his men. He ordered his brigade to keep a constant fire directed upon it. After several hours the tree began to waver. It finally fell, crushing several Confederates beneath it. Most of the day Upton, encouraging his men, rode back and forth just behind the firing line. He remained unhurt even after every member of his staff was either killed or wounded and he was the only mounted man in sight. At the Angle itself, the bayonet and stock were used by most of the men in preference to the Minié ball, as they seldom had time to load and little area in which to swing their rifles to aim.

In the middle of the afternoon Upton rode back to commandeer a section of guns. He returned with two fieldpieces from a regular battery, which he placed almost within arm's reach of the enemy. The gunners sent a double charge of canister through the Confederate ranks. At that range the cannon fire swept the trench. Moving their pieces closer, the gunners went to the top of the parapet and sent another charge plowing forward. By then all of the artillery horses were dead, and only two of the twenty-four men who manned the guns were still standing. The artillery fell silent. Finally Russell sent in reserves, and Upton's brigade, no longer even a respectable regiment in size, fell back.[18]

On the morning of May 14, Meade ordered Upton to cross the Ny River and seize Myers' Hill, to the left and front of the V Corps lines. When he arrived, Upton found that a regiment of regulars had already carried the hill, and he only had to relieve them. Setting up his command post in a house on top of the hill, Upton noticed a wood about 250 yards to his front and, to the right of it, about 800 yards away, another high hill, containing some Confederate infantry. To his left Upton saw a broad open field, on the far edge of which squads of enemy cavalry were forming for an attack. His brigade numbered only 800 men, because the state governors, anxious to provide commissions for as many of their political favorites as possible, created new regiments for recruits instead of reinforcing old, decimated units. Therefore Upton had to ask for reinforcements. Meade, who was on the hill with Upton, could bring up only two small regiments. Upton sent one of them forward to establish an outpost in the wood, but it encountered two Rebel brigades forming for a charge and fell back. The Rebels counterattacked, helped by a cavalry charge on Upton's left flank. Refusing his left, Upton stopped the advance. The Confederates outnumbered him, however, and when they regrouped and prepared to resume the advance, Upton decided that the risk of allowing Meade to be captured was too great and he fell back. That night, in a surprise attack, he regained the hill and held it for the next two days. He was soon pulled back, however, and his brigade spent the rest of May maneuvering as Grant attempted to get around Lee's flank. On May 24 Upton and his men tore up railroad tracks and destroyed them by removing the ties, stacking them with the rails on top, firing the wood, and bending the red hot rails around trees.[19]

At noon of June 1, after marching half the night, the brigade arrived opposite the Confederate works at Cold Harbor. Receiving orders to attack, Upton formed his men into a column of four lines, headed by the newly arrived Second Connecticut, a former artillery regiment converted to infantry and anxious to prove its mettle. The enemy had interlocking felled trees in front of his position. Emerging from a woods, the brigade charged across a clearing, only to be met by twin sheets of flame, one from the front and another from the left, where once again Upton was unsupported. So heavy was the fire that the air stank with sulphurous smoke and in sixty seconds 250 men were wounded or killed. "Lie down!" Upton yelled to his men.

"Murderous!" Upton later called the engagement. "We were recklessly ordered to assault the enemy's intrenchments knowing neither their strength nor position. Our loss was very heavy, and to no purpose. Our men are brave, but can not accomplish impossibilities."

Now Upton was trapped, his men frightened, cut off, and pinned down. He must rally them. "Put up your saber," he said to a young Connecticut officer. "I never draw mine until we get into closer quarters than this."

Turning to the men, Upton ordered them to cease firing and protect themselves. "See the Johnies! See the Johnies!" he shouted. "Boys, we'll have these fellows yet!"

When the Confederates turned their attention to the Union troops advancing on Upton's right, he extended his line to the left and ordered his brigade to begin firing again. The men were too shell-shocked to comply. To encourage them, Upton, whose horse had been killed, placed himself behind a tree in the extreme front and fired muskets as fast as the men could load and hand them to him. His firing drew a heavy return volley from the Confederates; Union troops began to sneak to the rear. Seeing them, Upton, who wanted to protect the brigade to his right (which had made some inroads into the enemy line), shouted, "Men of Connecticut, stand by me! We *must* hold this line."

Most of the men returned, and the line held. When a company commander sent word that if the Rebels charged he could not hold his position, Upton replied, "He must hold it. If they come, catch them on your bayonets, and pitch them over your heads!" The Second Connecticut suffered casualties of over 50 per cent that day, but it held.[20] The brigade maintained its tenuous position until the army left Cold Harbor. In the general charge of June 3, Upton and Russell agreed that an attack in their sector was impracticable and made none. After the fearful pounding the rest of the army took, they could hardly be criticized.

Criticism, in fact, was the other way around. "I am very sorry to say," Upton stated after Cold Harbor, "I have seen but little generalship during the campaign. Some of our corps commanders are not fit to be corporals." They were "lazy and indolent, refused to go to the front, knew nothing of conditions, yet, without hesitancy, they will order us to attack the enemy, no matter what their position or numbers." Only numbers, not generalship, could get the Army of the Potomac into Richmond. Upton thought Grant a great commander, but his immediate subordinates were "stumbling-blocks of too great magnitude to permit a brilliant execution of any movement in which they may be implicated. . . . I must confess that, so long as I see such incompetency, there is no grade in the army to which I do not aspire."[21]

The Second Brigade marched most of June before settling into the siege of Petersburg which proved a well-earned rest—neither Upton nor his men had taken off their clothes since the campaign began on May 4. Twice the men spent a day tearing up railroad tracks.[22] It had been a long campaign. Upton had learned much about war and he had earned his stars. His brigade had lost 329 killed, 713 wounded, and 236 missing, a total of 1.305 casualties, or more than 60 per cent. He came out of the holocaust with one major conclusion: Commanders up to and including divisional level must get in front of their men and lead them. The officers should not be reckless, but "it has now arrived at that point when officers must expose themselves freely if they would have their commands do their whole duty."[23] Soon he would be a division commander himself, and would have an opportunity to show that he meant what he said.

The Civil War: At the Top

Confident of his own abilities and eager for larger commands, Emory Upton, by June, 1864, was ready to take his place among the leading actors in the American drama. He watched anxiously as Lee, in an attempt to break Grant's strangle hold on Petersburg, sent Jubal Early's corps on a raid through the Valley of Virginia. Lee hoped that Grant would pull back from Petersburg to defend Washington; instead, the Union commander first ignored the threat, then sent only the VI Corps to the capital. Upton's brigade marched on July 10 to City Point, Virginia, and took transports to Washington. There it participated in the defensive actions around the capital until General Philip Sheridan assumed command of the forces in the area.

Sheridan, with three corps behind him, in September took the offensive to drive Early from the valley. By the 19th he had forced Early back to Front Royal, Virginia, and blue columns were preparing to cross the Opequan Creek, swing around Early's right flank on the Berryville Pike (thus cutting the Confederates off from Winchester), and force him to attack entrenched Union troops. The First Division of the VI Corps, to which Upton's brigade belonged, was on the right of the corps line. It connected with the left of General

George Crook's XIX Corps. The early morning march went
well, but when the Berryville Pike turned slightly to the left,
a gap opened between the right of the VI Corps and the left
of the XIX Corps. The gap increased in width as the troops
advanced. Early recognized both the danger to his flank and
the possibilities the divided Union forces presented. He
launched an attack on the XIX Corps while he rushed a
division into the gap separating the XIX and XI Corps. The
leftmost division of the XIX Corps, suffering from the attack
in its front and frightened by the presence of enemy troops
on its flank, broke and ran. Grasping the situation, Upton
shifted the front of his brigade, had the men lie down in a
protecting woods, and waited for more Confederates to
pour into the gap. When the trap was filled, he had his men
open a devastating fire. This, Upton reported, "caused the
enemy to retire in great disorder."

Springing to their feet, the men of the Second Brigade—
soon followed by others of the VI Corps—dashed after the
enemy, inflicting a heavy loss in killed and wounded. Upton's
action had averted probable disaster at the battle of the
Opequan.

Just before noon the division commander, General Russell,
was killed. At twenty-five years of age Upton became one of
the youngest division commanders in the Union army. He
had charge of and was responsible for three brigades and
thirteen regiments—more than 5,000 men. At the moment,
his force was not an impressive one, for the regiments and
brigades were badly mixed. Confused men were wandering
everywhere, looking for either their colors or a familiar face.
Any kind of coordinated action seemed impossible.

Upton decided that if he attempted to regroup his men
he would waste too much time. But he could not attack
until some order had been restored. Just as he was ready to
give up and lose his first opportunity to prove himself as a
division commander, Upton realized that he could straighten

his line without having to reorganize the men into their proper outfits. He had the men come forward to the edge of a wood, form into line, and dress their ranks. He told all officers to assume command of the appropriate number of men nearest him. Then he launched an attack. The Confederates fled from their positions, then tried to settle into new ones in the rear. Upton had his men move forward by leaps and bounds in an open order whenever the enemy fire slackened, but when it was heavy he halted the division and sent either the men on the left or right on a short flanking march. As soon as the Confederates shifted their attention to the flankers, the other brigades charged. By the middle of the afternoon the Union troops were making a general advance, driving the enemy from crest to crest. Upton rode at the head of his division, urging his men on.

Just then, a fragment of a bursting shell hit Upton. It tore his thigh muscle open and laid bare the femoral artery. Upton tumbled from his horse, blood spilling from his wound. Momentarily dazed, he oriented himself and looked up to see Sheridan standing over him and heard the general order him to the rear.

Upton was not going to give up his new command that easily. When Sheridan rode off, Upton called his staff surgeon to him and had the doctor stop the bleeding with a tourniquet. Then he demanded a stretcher and had himself borne about the field, while he gave orders to his brigade commanders. He did not leave the field until night quelled the battle.

It was a hard night for Upton, but the next morning the pain was allayed by the news that he had received a promotion to brevet major general of volunteers. In an army in which officers and men habitually quit fighting when they received the slightest wound, Upton's action was, to General James H. Wilson, "the most heroic . . . that came under my observation during the war." [1]

Soon after the battle Upton went home to Batavia to recover. He did some reading, kept up with military events
through the newspapers, and rested. The pain continued,
but it did not bother him as much as McClellan, who had
accepted the Democratic presidential nomination on a
"damnable platform," one which called for peace. Lincoln
had "made many gross blunders"—the Emancipation Proc-
lamation did not come soon enough to please the abolitionist Upton—"but he is true to his purpose." [2]

Eager to return to combat, Upton spent less time on the
Presidential campaign than he did following military events.
In November he noted that his fellow division commander
in the valley, General Wilson, had received orders from the
General-in-chief to assume command of the cavalry in the
West. Wilson arrived at Nashville, Tennessee, his headquar-
ters, just in time to participate in the battle there. After
General George H. Thomas' forces defeated those under
General John Bell Hood, Wilson's cavalry spent the next few
weeks in pursuit. This prevented Wilson from reorganizing
the cavalry corps until midwinter.

Wilson had been one year ahead of Upton at West Point,
graduating sixth in the class of 1860. The two young generals, both ambitious and self-confident, had been close
friends, and both had risen rapidly in the Union army. Wilson made his reputation in the western theater in the early
years of the war. In 1864 he went to Washington to head
the new Cavalry Bureau. In that position he learned of the
Spencer carbine, the first successful breech-loading, repeating, rifled carbine. Wilson thought the weapon ideal for
cavalry and did everything he could to arm cavalrymen with
it. In the Wilderness campaign, Wilson gave up his Washington post and served as commander of the Third Division
of the Cavalry Corps until he received his new post in the
West.

Wilson shared many of Upton's traits. Five feet, ten inches

tall, he looked taller because of his erect military bearing. Wilson was often blunt, even imperious. Bold and adventurous, he had supreme confidence in himself. He inspired those around him with the same confidence. A man of extremes, his commitment to and praise for a friend whom he trusted was complete, and he never wavered in his friendship and support.

When Grant gave Wilson his original orders, he promised the assistance of a few good officers from the Army of the Potomac. Wilson could make the selections. Upton, although not yet recovered from his wound, stood at the head of Wilson's list. As soon as he heard the news, Upton left Batavia and went to Nashville to assume command of the Fourth Division of the Cavalry Corps.

Upton limped into Wilson's headquarters and told his new superior "that he had no doubt of his professional capacity to manage cavalry as well as either artillery or infantry." Then he marched out to take a look at his men. Most of them were barely out of their teens, but they were all old soldiers. Fearful that they might not respect him, both because he was so young and because he came from the eastern theater, Upton informed the men of his intention to impose a strict discipline upon them. Soon he had them drilling daily, rain or shine, with and without the saber, mounted and dismounted. Upton's fears proved unfounded—the men were impressed. They did not hold his youth against him, and they had heard of his courage and skill in combat. To their delight, Upton thought up new evolutions for them, and they took pride in their skill. Upton in turn was overjoyed at his opportunity to reform cavalry organization and tactics.

One of the men, later to be Upton's clerk, described him. Slightly above medium stature, Upton rode a tall, long-bodied bay horse that made him appear smaller than he was. The general was keen-eyed and earnest about his work. He had a respectable library of military works in his tent and studied them every night. His voice was low and pleasant, but when excited he spoke rapidly. When "he gets angry he is quick as a flash, and the man he is talking to thinks a revolver is going off at him." And, to the astonishment of the westerners, "he says his prayers every night." [3]

Man for man, the force in which Upton served was the strongest on either side in the entire war. Armed principally with the repeating Spencer carbines (thanks to Wilson's insistence and perseverance), the 12,000 horsemen whom Wilson commanded were all veterans of arduous cavalry service. When they set out the men carried five-days' supply of bread and ten-days' supply of sugar and salt each, while the two hundred and fifty-wagon train contained forty-five-days' supply of coffee, twenty-days' ration of sugar, fifteen of salt, and eighty rounds of ammunition per man. A canvas pontoon train of thirty boats, transported by sixty-five six-mule teams under the escort of a battalion, completed the equipment.

Wilson's concept of the nature of his force—a concept with which Upton agreed—was relatively novel. Despite all lessons to the contrary, most eastern cavalry leaders in the first years of the war had tried to follow the European pattern of fighting with the saber from their horses. Wilson, Upton, and the overall commander in the West, General William T. Sherman, thought that on American terrain cavalry should ride to the scene of battle, then fight with rifles as dismounted infantry. In most of their battles the Cavalry Corps used this method. After one short, furious campaign Wilson told Sherman, "I regard this corps today as the model for modern cavalry in organization, armament, and discipline, and hazard nothing in saying that it embodies more of the virtues of the three arms, without any sacrifice of those of cavalry, than any similar number of men in the world." Reminding Sherman of some previous uncomplimentary remarks he had made about the Union cavalry, Wilson continued: "From an undisciplined mob [the Cavalry Corps] has taken the most perfect discipline; from fragments of every variety it has taken a most coherent organization. The spirit of the men is magnificent, the officers are admirable, and think their corps invincible." [4]

Wilson's task was twofold. Starting from the vicinity of Florence, Alabama, he was to move toward Selma, the industrial center of the state, and toward General Nathan Bedford Forrest and his 12,000 cavalry. The Union cavalry set out on March 22, 1865, with Upton's division in the lead. Wilson trusted Upton because the two men understood each other. During the campaign they acted more like twin commanders than superior and subordinate. Wilson usually gave Upton the lead on the march and allowed him to make his own decisions, because Wilson knew that Upton would react to a situation the same as he would.

By March 28, Upton had reached the Cahawba River, near Elyton, but was unable to get more than one regiment across because of high water caused by heavy rain, and because Forrest had placed obstructions in the ford. The next day, Wednesday, he made little progress as the rains continued, but by Thursday morning he was across before the other two divisions arrived. While they crossed, Upton destroyed iron works, rolling mills, and collieries in the area—industries which were the main source of supply for the arsenals, foundries, and navy yard at Selma. On March 31 Upton rode through Montevallo, in north central Alabama. He encountered General Philip D. Roddey, who was coming up from Selma in order to slow Wilson's march until Forrest's forces could be concentrated against the Union troops. Leaving a line of dismounted skirmishers about one mile to the south and hiding the bulk of his troops north of Montevallo, Upton withdrew into the village. Roddey attacked the skirmish line and drove it back; when it was within a

few hundred yards of the village Upton called up his main
body, which rode in columns of fours at a trot through the
village, then broke into a gallop. It forced the enemy back
and captured fifty prisoners. When Roddey set up a defensive line on the opposite side of a creek, Upton sent one
brigade around his left flank while he unlimbered a battery
of artillery and opened a frontal fire. Fighting of a similar
nature occupied the remainder of the day, with Roddey
falling back.[5]

On April 1 Upton's division pursued Roddey as far as
Randolph, north of Selma. There Upton took a road leading
to the left in an effort to outflank Roddey, and to clear the
main road to Selma for the two following Union divisions.
Cutting back to the right on a road that intersected the main
Selma road at Ebenezer Church, Upton struck enemy forces
under the command of Forrest himself. Upton dismounted
one brigade and set it on a frontal attack. Another still
mounted brigade worked around Forrest's flank. The Confederates fell back, leaving their guns and 300 prisoners.

That night Wilson's force camped at Plantersville, nineteen miles north of Selma. As Upton relaxed in the darkness
one of his men brought him an English civil engineer who
had been employed on the fortifications at Selma and who
had surrendered. At Upton's request, the engineer made a
pencil sketch of the works and topography, together with
the number and position of the guns, around Selma. Upton
took it to Wilson, and the two officers discussed the situation.

Forrest had surrounded Selma with a well-constructed,
bastioned line of earthworks and stockades that extended in
a semicircle around the city and connected at each end with
the banks of the Alabama River. He had covered the major
roads leading into the city with a second line of works. He
had protected the thirty-two guns and the main line of
defense with a stockade of stakes five and a half feet high

and from six to eight inches thick, planted in the ground and sharpened at the top. The guns swept the cultivated land around the works. Forrest had gathered all his men inside the defense to protect the city, which by now contained the South's principal gun factory, armory, machine shops, and manufacturing establishments.

After more than an hour's deliberation, Wilson and Upton decided to leave all impediments behind, march to the city in the late afternoon, and launch at dusk a two-pronged attack with dismounted troops. Upton would make his attack on the left while General Eli Long, whose division was heavier by two regiments, would attack on the right. Since Upton had unusual experience with attacks of this nature, Wilson would stay with Long on the right. The plan proved to be as effective as it was simple. When Upton heard sounds of battle on his right, he urged his men forward. They arrived before the stockade with only minor casualties. Finding the obstructions too difficult to break down or pry away, Upton's men stormed the works by playing "leapfrog." The leading men bent down and those following jumped on their shoulders and over the stockade. Once on the other side, they scattered the Confederates, then opened a pass in the stockade, through which Upton's reserve brigade—still mounted—rode. The federal horsemen spread out behind the enemy's lines in various directions and captured some artillery and hundreds of prisoners. The battle of Selma was a complete success for Wilson and Upton. For the first time in the war Union soldiers had defeated Forrest—who had nearly as many men as Wilson—in a fair fight.[6]

Wilson, his major missions completed with the capture of Selma and the destruction of Forrest, became a free agent. Now he could either march south to Mobile and join General Edward R. Canby, or he could move eastward and unite with Sherman. Agreeing with Upton that Mobile would fall to Canby without their aid, he decided to move eastward.

The cavalry set out on April 10. That afternoon Upton, in the lead, came to a small creek with steep, slippery clay bluffs on the east bank. A Confederate cavalry brigade on the opposite side opened fire, and Upton motioned his men to fall back. He glanced at the bank and saw that it extended as far north and south as he could see; much valuable time could be lost hunting for a safe crossing. Upton conferred with his bugler and orderly. They rode away to the north. A few silent minutes followed.

Suddenly Upton galloped forward, brandishing his sword. "They are flanking them on the left," he yelled. "Forward!" The ruse worked. The Confederates, hearing Upton's bugler to their right "blowing for all he was worth, and his orderly raising the devil among the corn-stalks . . . lit out of there like a flock of wild ducks." [7]

On April 12 the Union cavalry marched through an undefended Montgomery. Upton was in the van, and it fell to him to secure a bridgehead over the Chattahoochee River, the boundary between Alabama and Georgia. On April 16 he arrived in front of Columbus, Georgia, a fortified city on the east bank of the river. Three bridges crossed the river around Columbus, one a foot bridge at the lower end of the city and the others foot and railroad bridges three-fourths of a mile upriver. The Confederates had protected the lower bridge with a riflepit and three pieces of artillery on the east bank. At the upper bridges they had two redoubts connected by riflepits on the west bank. The lower redoubt contained six twelve-pounder howitzers and four ten-pounder Parrotts; the upper redoubt had fourteen guns, two of which were howitzers. The riflepits held 2,700 infantrymen.

Upton arrived before the lower bridge about 2 P.M. and immediately charged it. Heavy artillery and musketry fire held him up while the Confederates burned the bridge. Meanwhile Wilson arrived. Upton, after explaining the situation, said he would like to swing to the north, charge the upper works with dismounted infantry, then pass cavalry through the gap and secure a bridge. "But," Upton concluded, shading his eyes from the setting sun, "it is now too late. It will be dark before I can get into position and lead the division to the attack." Wilson, however, decided that a night attack on a strong position was preferable—this was the lesson from Selma—and told Upton to make his attack at 8:30 P.M.

"Do you mean it? It will be dark as midnight by that hour and that will be a night attack, indeed."

Wilson assured him that he was serious, and Upton exclaimed, "By jingo, I'll do it; and I'll sweep everything before me."

After gulping down his rations, Upton rode north to attack the works protecting the upper bridges. Dismounting one of his two remaining brigades, he sent it against the riflepits, which it carried. But he did not know that this was merely the outermost and weakest of two lines of entrenchments. Still a gap had been made, and the bluecoated cavalry swept forward. In the second line of works the Confederates, confused by the darkness and the noise, thought that the galloping horsemen were southerners. They allowed Upton's men to pass unchallenged through their lines, over the bridge, and into the city. Meanwhile, some of Upton's dismounted troops pushed forward and became engaged in a fire fight with the second line, while others charged the redoubts to their right and left.

"Charge 'em!" Upton kept shouting. "Charge 'em!" The mounted troops heard his commotion and, after disposing of the fifty-man guard at the foot bridge and securing it from possible burning, recrossed and rejoined the main body. They spread panic as they rode by pouring a deadly fire into the enemy's lines. After a short fight the redoubts and the second line of works fell. The federals rushed forward, shouting "Selma! Selma! Go for the bridge! Waste no time with prisoners!" Passing into Columbus, they spread out through the city and attacked the forces protecting the upper railroad trestle and the lower bridge. By 10 P.M. Columbus, 1,500 prisoners, and 24 guns were in Upton's possession, at cost of 30 Union troops killed and wounded. Upton had won a complete and devastating victory at the battle of Columbus.[8]

Yet, for Upton and Wilson, the war was over. On April 20 Upton, striking out alone, occupied Macon without resistance. Lee's surrender at Appomattox earlier in the month had effectively brought a halt to the war. Only mopping-up operation remained. Wilson gave Upton the task of marching on Augusta, Georgia, to receive the surrender of Confederate troops there and take general command of the city. He was ordered to restore peace and good order by forcing editors to publish their newspapers "in the interests of peace . . . and national unity," and by prohibiting all public meetings.[9] Arriving in Augusta on May 5, Upton carried out his orders, then informed Wilson that Jefferson Davis, with $6,000,000 in gold, was attempting to escape to the Trans-Mississippi. Davis was supposed to be in north Georgia. Wilson told Upton to use any means necessary to capture the Confederate president; Upton printed and distributed posters offering a $100,000 reward for information leading to his arrest. Elements of Wilson's cavalry soon caught Davis.[10]

A much more difficult task for Upton came when he hoisted the American flag over the United States Arsenal at Augusta. He had to make a suitable speech: "Four years ago the Governor of Georgia, at the head of an armed force, hauled down the American flag at this Arsenal. The President of the United States called the nation to arms to repossess the forts and arsenals that had been seized. After four years of sanguinary war and conflict, we execute the order of the great preserver of the Union and liberty, and to-day we again hoist the Stars and Stripes over the Arsenal at Augusta.

Majestically, triumphantly, she rises." [11] The crowd cheered.

Upton spent most of the rest of the month of May making arrests and seizures. His men caught Alexander H. Stephens in Columbus and started the Confederate Vice President on his journey to prison. Upton took possession of the assets of the Bank of Tennessee, which were in Augusta, arrested some still disloyal editors, and generally engaged in the occupation duties which have so often been the lot of the United States Army—duties for which neither he nor any other officer in the army had any training.

Upton's orientation was still towards making war, not— as with his men—reducing the size of the army and mustering out of the service. When he discovered on May 13 that a Confederate cavalry force had surrendered some fine horses at Resaca, Upton asked permission to use some of the money taken from the Bank of Tennessee to buy the mounts for his division. Wilson refused.[12] The men were already beginning to leave the service. As fast as the administration could muster them out, regiments went home. On May 26 the Tenth Missouri Cavalry left. Its colonel, in behalf of the regiment, told Upton he was sorry to leave, but the prospect of peace took away "the sting of separation." The war over, the men would return to their usual pursuits. "In conclusion, receive from us a farewell the bitterness of which is sweetened by our bright prospects for the future." Upton had to stand by and watch the finest cavalry force in the world disband before his eyes.[13]

In early June the division broke up. In a farewell address, Upton expressed his "high appreciation of the bravery, endurance, and soldierly qualities" displayed by the men. "Whether mounted with the saber or dismounted with the carbine," the division "triumphed over the enemy in every conflict. You will return to your homes," Upton concluded, "with the proud consciousness of having defended the flag of your country in the hour of the greatest national peril, while through your instrumentality liberty and civilization will have advanced the greatest stride recorded in history." [14]

The Cavalry Corps was gone. It had been a great force, and a cocky one. Wilson said that the officers and men "felt that nothing was impossible to them. Relying on their Spencers, . . . and their splendid horse artillery always close up with the skirmish line, they . . . justly regarded themselves equal to any task that might fall to their lot." [15] After the capture of Columbus, Upton told Wilson that "he could traverse the Confederacy from end to end, and from side to side, with his single division, carrying any kind of fortifications by assault . . . and defying capture by any kind or amount of force which might be sent against him." [16]

Upton would always remember his cavalry service with fondness. Thirteen years after the war, he told a visitor from his old division that he "would like to commute the rest of his life for six months of just such military service." [17] Just as the Civil War was the central theme of American history, it was the central theme in Upton's life. Nothing he had done before could compare with it, and nothing that happened to him afterwards could dim the memory of those glorious, tragic—and, for him, happy—days. Emory Upton had gone off to war at twenty-one and before his twenty-fifth birthday he had risen to major general. The praise and rewards he received gave him an unlimited confidence in his own abilities. His success as a tactical reformer made him eager to continue his activities in that area.

But Upton could never forget what he had seen in the Civil War—volunteers refusing to fight because their contracts had been violated; professional soldiers pushed aside for political favorites; state governors withholding promotions from deserving men; incompetents, both professional and amateur, in command of army corps; militiamen running from the banks of Bull Run. The Civil War, the great experience in his life, taught Upton that the military policy of the United States needed improvement. The great crusade had been successfully completed—now other crusades had to be found. First in tactical reform, then in general military policy, Upton would find them.

But the immediate future contained only drudgery and careful bookkeeping, the traditional duties of the peacetime army. Upton would have to adjust to a new life. His Civil War career demonstrated that he should be capable of making the adjustment. "General Upton," one observer said of him in 1865, "is a thorough student of military science, and is also a master of the details of military life. He is quick to see and use the material at hand to accomplish his designs." Moreover, he "has the enthusiasm of youth, but he is not rash; he has inordinate ambition, but is neither selfish nor cringing; he believes in himself, yet is neither over-confident nor vain." [18]

Summarizing the opinion of many officers about the young man who had successfully commanded in all three arms of the service, Wilson said Upton "was incontestably the best tactician of either army. . . . So long as the Union has such soldiers as he to defend it, it will be perpetual." [19] But, for Upton, making war had come easily and naturally; now his task was the more difficult one of proving himself in the peacetime army.

Postwar

Only twenty-six years old when the war ended, Upton feared that his days of greatness were over. Up to 1865 things had come easily for the young soldier, but now he found himself on the lower rungs of a traditionally despised and consistently neglected peacetime army. He was determined to fight his way upward, but a deep personal tragedy, plus public indifference to the internal affairs of the army, made progress difficult. By 1870 he had scarcely improved his position, but he had established a strong base from which he could move forward.

In July, 1865, Upton went to Lenoir, Tennessee, to take command of the cavalry of the District of East Tennessee. By August 15 he had gathered up the Confederate arms in the area and completed his paroling duties, and he received orders from the War Department to report to General John Pope, Department of the Missouri.[1] Before he left, Upton had a talk with Wilson, who was thinking of resigning from the army in order to engage in railroad construction. Wilson contended that it was as honorable for a man to leave the army in peacetime as it was to enter it in war and urged Upton to resign also. Upton considered the proposition, but declined. He realized, he said, that his campaigning days were over, but he felt there was still an opportunity for him in the army as an authority on tactics.[2]

When Upton arrived at departmental headquarters in St. Louis, Pope gave him the command of the District of Colorado, with headquarters at Denver. On August 31 he left Fort Leavenworth, Kansas, with one other officer, two wagons, and two mules. The trip was a long and, on the whole, pleasant one. After two unsuccessful attempts, he killed a buffalo. Throughout the countryside he enjoyed the scenery. On the evening of September 29 he arrived in Denver, a six-year-old city with a population of 4,000. He was astonished at the inflation on the frontier—board at the hotels began at $135 a month—and found the citizens "not so polished as Eastern people," although he did meet "many nice gentlemen."[3] A mining boom was on in the territory, and speculation, claim jumping, and general crime were rampant.

Pope's orders to Upton were simple and direct—he should retrench. Pope wanted Upton to reduce the forces and expenditures in Colorado "to the utmost extent consistent with absolute necessity." All unnecessary troops should be mustered out of the service, all extra officers sent back to St. Louis, and all excessive supplies either stored or sold. "I cannot too strongly impress upon you," Pope concluded, "the absolute necessity of reducing troops and expenditures . . . at the earliest possible moment."[4] Upton was beginning to realize what normal life in the army was like.

He threw himself into the task. After one day in Denver, he left on a two-week tour of his command. During the war he had been too busy as a combat commander to learn anything about the extent of the corruption which was so much a part of the business of supplying the army; what he discovered in Colorado shocked him. "I find myself surrounded by a set of unscrupulous contractors," he informed Pope, "who regard the public money as their legitimate plunder."

To effect retrenchment in the face of the well-nigh universal corruption would be difficult, and Upton expected "to call down on my head the venom of the entire class." But he was determined to "defeat their villainous schemes." All he asked was the support of his superiors. He received it, and by December he had reformed his command.[5]

As soon as he had his duties as district commander down to administrative details, Upton turned his attention to a more serious and interesting problem. In the post–Civil War American army there was a great interest in tactical reform. Professional soldiers agreed that the war had numerous lessons to teach, lessons which had to be assimilated to the army's tactical drill. Upton wanted to be the man who would put those lessons down on paper in a coherent form and thus bring tactical systems another step forward.

Since the overthrow of the mounted, armored knight, tactics had been in a constant state of flux. The bayonet, which with the invention of the ring bayonet in 1678 became a practical weapon, eliminated the need for pikemen to protect infantry from cavalry. It thus made possible the line of infantry, which could produce a much heavier fire than a column or square (needed for protection from cavalry before the bayonet) and so was a preferable offensive formation. Linear tactics, which dominated the eighteenth-century battlefield, were designed to exploit the new fire power to the fullest through the simultaneous volley. They left no room for individual initiative. Soldiers had to march in step, so that all could fire at once, which was the reason for the Prussian goose step, a most practical device for keeping the lines straight. Indeed, Prussian officers were reputed to dress their companies with surveying instruments. Linear tactics reduced the potentialities of an army, because the huge frontage of a linear body of men required a broad and reasonably level plain to mount an attack. Battle could be joined only if both commanders were confident, because a general could refuse an engagement merely by withdrawing to nearby woods or hills. And despite the heavy losses due to murderous exchanges of volleys—often as high as 50 per cent—victories were seldom complete, since the line could not be adapted to relentless pursuit.[6]

There were other difficulties involved in a linear attack. The men had to be well drilled to keep in step and well disciplined to hold their position while they received a volley from the defenders. Moreover, the second, third, and fourth lines always had the obstacle of dead bodies to cross, which threw individuals out of line. The French, whose raw revolutionary levies could not be trained to stand up in line and fire volleys, were the first to present a solution. For their infantry assaults the French employed the column until the last possible moment then deployed into a line. (Columns were impractical for the final attack because the men were exposed to flank fire, and those in the rear could not fire for fear of hitting their comrades in front, so the column could not mount a volley.) This made it easier for their troops to reach the battle quickly, while retaining the advantage of fire power inherent in a final linear attack. To protect the advancing columns the French used skirmishers, individuals or pairs of men who moved ahead of the main body and fired from cover. The harassment of the skirmishers prevented the defenders from standing and throwing a unified volley into the attacking column.[7]

In Napoleon's time the ordinary infantry weapon was a muzzle-loading smoothbore musket, a piece which was inaccurate and had an effective range of only fifty yards. Commanders never encouraged individual marksmanship among troops using the smoothbores, but rather relied on the volley. After Napoleon's overthrow the development of a new bullet, a conical projectile with a hollow or brass base which could expand to take the grooves in a barrel and thus leave the piece with a spin (which kept the bullet true to its course), made the rifle an effective infantry weapon. For the first time the rifle could be loaded as fast as the smoothbore. Moreover, the spin imparted to the bullet—called, after its inventor, the Minié ball—by rifling increased not only the accuracy but also the range of infantry fire. This helped strengthen the defense, which could now fire at will and with great effect at a range of over 200 yards, raising havoc with a linear attack. Another advantage was the copper cap ignition system, which made the rifle reliable even in bad weather.

Rifling also revolutionized the artillery. Napoleon had used his artillery to smash the enemy with case shot from outside musket range—grape shot and canister were deadly at about twice the effective range of the smoothbore—but the rifle forced the artillery to fall back to ranges where it had to use solid shot. In 1862, in Virginia, Upton had found that exploding shells, when used from great distances, were unreliable, and had switched to solid shot. The latter, however, usually did small damage to infantry. Therefore most artillery commanders, especially when they were on the defensive, saved their powder and case until the enemy charged, which forced the attacking infantry to take on both opposing infantry and artillery firing shrapnel. This was another clear gain for the defense, because the offensive artillery was unable to make its weight felt.[8] For example, Lee's artillery at Gettysburg, throwing solid shot into the Union lines, did little damage, while Meade's artillery, waiting for the infantry charge, used shrapnel and canister and tore gaping holes in Pickett's lines.

Because no great wars occurred between the overthrow of Napoleon and the American Civil War, these lessons had not been recognized, much less accepted, by professional soldiers. Still, they did experiment. At the battle of the Alma, in the Crimean War, the British tried an advance in three lines on a front of two miles. The Russians, grouped

in dense columns and firing at will, broke the formation easily, but when they tried to counterattack with the columns,
thinking to deploy into a line at the moment of contact, the
fire of the British line drove them off. The action showed
both that a long rigid line was not the best formation for
an attack and that heavy columns took too long to deploy
and so could be destroyed before completing their maneu-
ver.[9] The solution seemed to be to send skirmishers out
ahead of light columns, which could then be deployed when
needed to develop fire power. Most Americans, however,
including the official observer, George B. McClellan, missed
the lesson. In the Civil War they continued to rely on the
long, rigid line.[10] Upton, at Spotsylvania and later in the
West as a cavalry commander, was one of the first to break
out of the pattern.

Other American soldiers did make adjustments. They
began to use skirmishers extensively. By 1865 the rifled
musket had forced the generals to stretch their battle lines,
form their armies for combat much farther apart than
formerly, reduce the density of men in the battle zone, and
accept the fire fight rather than the bayonet charge as decisive.[11] Europeans realized the same things. Sir Patrick
MacDougall, a British observer, interpreted the Civil War
to mean that the increased efficiency of the rifle would force
infantry to adopt less rigid and more extended battle formations.[12]

Many Civil War soldiers saw the need and in a haphazard
way adapted their tactics to the changed situation, but few
were prepared to do the arduous work necessary to create
a new, formal tactical system. Upton was. As early as the
Wilderness campaign he spent spare moments trying to
work out a new drill system which would allow the attackers
to bring a maximum fire power to bear while exposing themselves as little as possible. In the West, he continued the
work, and began to make allowance for the breech-loader

and the repeater, both of which he saw used there on a mass scale for the first time. The breech-loader had two great advantages: it could be loaded faster, and could be loaded from the prone position. Upton realized immediately that it was the weapon of the future (others did not; Robert E. Lee thought the men would waste ammunition using it), and based his tactical system on its use.

Upton kept a clerk busy copying down his ideas, formations, and movements. Once, during a break, the clerk told him of a company of militia which he had seen drilling in Missouri. When ordering a right wheel, the captain would shout, "Break in two and swing round like a gate!" Upton laughed, then remarked that it had the advantage of simplicity.[13]

In Colorado, after he eliminated the corruption, Upton devoted himself to his tactical system. By January, 1866, he felt he was well enough along to request permission to go to Washington in order to submit his system to a board of general officers for adoption by the army. In the request, Upton outlined his system. The feats of dismounted cavalry armed with the Spencer carbine demonstrated the necessity for a one-rank tactical line to replace the old three-rank system, which dated back to eighteenth-century French tactics. Men armed with breech-loaders could keep up a continuous fire and need never step to the rear to reload, so one rank was sufficient. The single rank would reduce casualties. Previously, all American tactics had been based on the French system evolved in the eighteenth century. Upton eliminated the French facings and inversions, necessary in three-rank tactics, and substituted for them wheeling by "fours," the key to his drill. Upton divided a company into groups of four men and treated each group as a single unit with its own numerical designation. This allowed captains to form their line in any direction "with utmost facility and ease" by ordering the "fours" forward, left, or right. He simplified the French system by reducing the number of commands and introducing greater uniformity among them. But the important innovation was that the principle of fours allowed troops to come on the field either in column or in two or three ranks, then through a simple command expand or deploy into a single rank. It thus facilitated the use of skirmishers, who would assume an increasingly important role in Upton's thinking. Later Upton's fours would be called a squad, but his basic system continued to dominate army tactics.[14]

By February, Upton felt he was finished. He told his sister Sara, "I have had quite a play-spell for the past week." He looked forward to adoption by the War Department and thought that success would give him a solid reputation. But in April he confessed that the plates, illustrating the movements, were giving him trouble. "Were my tactics but a revision of the present system," he said, "with a few unimportant movements added, I would not be sanguine, but as they aim at a complete revolution, and are far more simple, my confidence increases with every comparison I make." If the tactics were not adopted, he would finance publication himself.

In late April, 1866, as a result of Congressional reduction in the size of the army, Upton was mustered out of the volunteer service. He had hoped for a colonel's commission in the regular army, but instead received a lieutenant-colonelcy in the Twenty-fifth United States Infantry. Still, the change in status did get him out of Colorado, and he lost no time in going to Washington, where he urged the War Department to create a board to examine his tactics. The Department agreed to do so, and on June 5 appointed a board to meet at West Point.[15] Upton was ordered to join the board at the Academy. During the war, he had avoided

an appointment to West Point, but now, when the alterna-
tive was service on the plains with the Twenty-fifth Infantry,
he accepted.

Upton spent the next year at West Point, training the
cadets in his system and displaying the results to the board.
He told his former classmate Henry du Pont that he was
confident of adoption, that the Point was "looking beauti-
fully," and that he was having a good time.[16] For Upton, it
was an ideal situation. He was an important figure in a key
reform in the institution he identified with and loved. All
of his needs were being answered—his ambition, his drive to
better the world, and his craving for an orderly, disciplined
life.

In January, 1867, the board reported unanimously to
adopt Upton's system. General-in-chief Grant, in advising
Secretary of War Edwin Stanton of the report, recommended
an immediate adoption by the army. "I have seen the system applied to company and battalion drills," he said, "and
am fully satisfied of its superior merits and adaptability to
our service; besides, it is no translation, but a purely American work." But opposition arose, and before committing itself the War Department appointed another board, with
Grant, Meade, and Edward Canby as members, to examine
Upton's system. In July, 1867, the new board also recommended adoption, pointing out that the advantages of Upton's system included the ease with which it could be applied to all arms of the service, its simplicity, which would
allow volunteer troops to learn it quickly, and its superior
system of providing for single-rank fighting and skirmishing. Further, it increased the number of methods of passing
from column to line while facing in any direction and diminished the time required for such changes. On August 1,
1867, through General Orders No. 73, the War Department
adopted the new system for the United States Army and
the militia of the United States.[17]

Upton copied the bulk of his *Infantry Tactics* from Silas Casey's earlier work on the same subject. The school of the soldier—including his position at attention, at ease, and at rest, his exercises, salutes, facings, bayonet drill, firing, and target practice—came directly from Casey, who had copied from the French. The same was true for the material on camping, ceremonies, trumpet signals, and drum and fife signals.[18] Upton was most interested in a new tactical response to the introduction of the breech-loader. In his preface he noted that the breech-loader would not change the principles of grand tactics, for although it would give a great impetus to the employment of skirmishers, still the safety of an army could not be entrusted to men in open order, but must rest on a line or lines of battle to support or receive an attack. Although attacks in masses, either by heavy column or rigid line, must be abandoned in the face of the rapid firing breech-loader, nevertheless "a preponderance of men and of fire" would still be the key to carrying a defensive position. The rapidity and ease with which a line of battle could be extended by means of throwing out more skirmishers—and it was there that Upton's system made its greatest contribution—made flanking movements difficult, but he added the caveat that "the extension of the line carries with it the danger of being pierced, which is more disastrous." [19]

In his skirmish drill, the heart of the system, Upton attempted to adjust to American topography. He had noticed that in the Atlanta campaign of 1864 troops rarely engaged in direct battle. Rather, due to the wooded and hilly nature of the terrain, most of the fighting was done by heavy skirmishers, a body whose importance Upton always emphasized.[20]

Upton described a new, special training for skirmishers. In his system officers impressed on each man the idea of his individuality and responsibility—the old days of the dull, unimaginative soldier who fired, without aiming, when told, were gone. The men learned to economize their strength, fire only at a target, and take advantage of all available cover, while the officers cultivated among them the idea that they could not be beaten. Upton's emphasis upon individual responsibility was a compensation for the loss of communications which his open order brought about. The greatest advantage of the old close order tactical system was that it allowed the commander to make his orders known to his men. Under Upton's system, with its emphasis on skirmishing, the commander would lose most or all of his control, as the men would be either out of sight or beyond the range of his voice. To compensate for the loss, Upton stressed individual responsibility.

Upton designed his battalion attack to take advantage of his skirmishers' abilities. He divided the battalion into two parts, one the fighting line, composed of two companies, the first serving immediately as skirmishers, the second as supports, and a reserve line composed of the two remaining companies. Skirmishers moved forward by leaps and bounds, keeping up a harassing fire. As they approached the defense line, officers fed more men into the skirmish line. The men moved forward by fours, each group having a number so that the captain could call it up at will. The reserves, in column, followed the advance of the skirmishers. When the skirmishers were within 150 yards of the position, and the reserves were 200 or so yards away, one company of the reserves deployed from column into line and charged. If it could not carry the position, the second company deployed into line and charged past it, the two companies advancing by leaps and bounds until the position fell. "The object to be kept steadily in view with the breech-loading tactics," Upton summarized, "is to shake the *morale* of the enemy by securing in every stage of the advance a preponderating fire, at the same time advancing in such small fractions, up to the moment of the final rush or assault, as to reduce the casualties to the lowest limit." As a general statement on the nature of modern tactics, Upton's summary was still valid in the mid-twentieth century.

There was little difference between Upton's system and that of the most important European tactician of the period. Colonel Charles J. Ardant du Picq, of the French army, was simultaneously coming to the same conclusions Upton had reached. None of Ardant du Picq's work was published before his death in 1870; later it would have an immense influence on European tactics, practically dominating French thought until after World War I. Like Upton, Ardant du Picq emphasized the moral factor in modern war, with special reference to skirmishers. "It is this class of fire, indeed," Ardant du Picq believed, "which is deadliest in war." [21]

Both Upton and Ardant du Picq were breaking with tradition, and both found acceptance difficult. In the American army, Upton's book raised a storm. For years *The Army and Navy Journal*, semiofficial and highly respected organ of the armed forces, carried criticisms. One officer, missing the point, complained that of the 2,147 paragraphs in Upton's work, 1,428 of them were copied from Casey. He thought the whole thing should be thrown out. A critic of Upton's style was appalled because "the action of grasping the small of the stock with the right hand is expressed in eight ways," and "the left hand drops by the side, sometimes 'quickly,' sometimes 'smartly,' and sometimes without qualification." Another, more perceptive officer, was aware of what Upton was trying to accomplish, but thought the division into fours and the numbering of each group would lead to mass confusion in battle, because with each casualty the men would have to be renumbered. "The hotter the fire the oftener a fellow's number would change," and it was unreasonable to expect that in the heat of battle men would remember their constantly changing arbitrary numerical designation. "Keno-callers would make good captains for this sort of business," he remarked.[22]

The editor of the *Journal*, William Conant Church, supported Upton. He thought the use of four men as a unit admirable, and was pleased because Americans finally had their own, and not a borrowed, system of tactics. Church soon made Upton the tactical editor of the *Journal*.[23]

Upton had other matters which drew his attention away from the praise, and criticism, of his *Tactics*. In 1865, before he left Tennessee to go to Colorado, Upton had gone to Knoxville to visit an old comrade from the Selma campaign, General Andrew J. Alexander. The General had married Evelina Martin, and she and Upton became good friends. Mrs. Alexander invited Upton to visit her at her family home at Willowbrook, on the eastern shore of Lake Owasco in New York. Upon his return from Colorado, Upton went to Willowbrook, where he found the Martins giving a party and the Alexanders absent. Embarrassed—he knew none of the company—he turned to walk away. Twenty-one-year-old Emily Martin noticed him and came down the porch steps to greet him. Upton explained why he was there; Emily excused herself from the company and took him for a walk along Lake Owasco. The next January they met in New York and toured the city together.

Emily was a handsome woman, with a delicate, rounded chin, full lips, a strong, straight nose, and rather large, attractive eyes. Upton, despite his years of active soldiering, had no experience with women, and was both drawn to and cowed by Emily. She in turn was attracted to him as a lost soul that needed saving. His experiences in the Civil War and in Colorado, where he had seen many dishonest men advance, had shaken his faith. Emily had made her profession of faith when she was twelve years old, and scattered through her diary prayers that God would teach her "to be gentle," and "to be kind," and "to be obliging," and "to do more good to others." Soon after meeting Upton, she began to concentrate on redeeming him. Her hopes were high, because her brother-in-law General Alexander had informed her of his "decided stand on the Lord's side while at the Point." She told Upton, "Never was I more shocked and astonished than when I heard from your own lips the admission that your faith in God's justice had been shaken, and that you no longer felt that you were a Christian." She urged him to return to the "blessedness of being a child of God." [24] He heeded her entreaties, and returned to the fold.

In November, 1867, Upton took a year's leave of absence. He set out for Willowbrook, to lay siege to Emily's heart. He reported to Wilson that although "the flanks were well protected and a heavy line of skirmishers concealed completely all assailable approaches in front," he was encouraged by the booty to be gained, and in a short but furious attack succeeded "in carrying the breastwork." On November 16 Emory and Emily became engaged, and Upton spent the Christmas season at Willowbrook.[25] They were married on February 19, 1868, at Willowbrook. Among the officers in attendance were Alexander, Du Pont, and Wilson. In March the couple sailed for Europe and toured France and Italy— Upton's royalties on his *Tactics* amounted to more than $1,000 per year—before Emily contracted an infection in her lungs. She needed Upton's constant care throughout the rest of the trip. He took her to specialists, but they could not find a cure. In August the Uptons returned to New York, then in October went to Key West. They hoped the climate there would help Emily's lungs.

Soon Upton had to return to active duty with his regiment, stationed at Memphis, and he left Emily with her sister Nelly. For five months he lived without her, but he had professional cares to occupy his mind.[26] He continued to dabble in his tactical system and looked forward to a possible ap-

pointment as Commandant of Cadets at West Point—a position traditionally occupied by an expert in tactics, because
the commandant had charge of Cadet drill. His immediate
plans were to read as much military history as possible. He
thought West Point needed an infusion of young blood in its
faculty, because the older professors were ignoring the
strategical and tactical lessons of the Civil War, and he
wanted to prepare himself in case he received an appointment on the teaching staff at the Academy.[27] He seized on
Wilson's life of Grant, published in 1868, and praised the
author for his honest account.[28]

A Union officer and abolitionist, Upton was a staunch
Republican. He greeted Grant's election to the Presidency,
"the recent Vicksburg to the rebel Democracy," with enthusiasm. Democrats, he noted, were down in the mouth, and he
predicted they would continue to be as long as they opposed
the "spirit of our institutions. . . . What a glorious era is now
before us!" he exulted. "The results of the war secured, the
national candidate established, and peace restored." Upton
reported that he lost a hat because of the election, "occa-
sioned by protruding my toe through it when I heard that
Grant was elected." [29]

In March, 1869, Upton's regiment went to Atlanta, and
he told Emily to pack her things and join him there. The
Georgia climate, he thought, would be just right for her
lungs. He met her in New Orleans, where they had a reunion
before going on to McPherson Barracks in Atlanta where
Emily set up housekeeping.

Upton had given something less than a total emotional
commitment to his marriage. The entire love affair contained
all the elements of a stylized, set piece carried out in strict
accordance with the rigorous demands of the Victorian era—
boy loses faith, meets girl, she restores faith, they marry.
Upton knew nothing of love beyond what he had read in

occasional magazine romances, and Emily was too young and too much of a religious zealot to be an experienced person capable of emotional involvement. The two recited speeches to each other during their courtship; during the honeymoon Emily was ill; afterwards they did not see each other. They hardly knew one another.

At Atlanta they fell in love. It was the happiest period of Upton's life. He worked hard during the day, then went home and spent the evenings talking and laughing with Emily. They explored each others interests and hopes for the future. On Sundays they attended church together, as well as prayer meetings during the week. Emily took great interest in Upton's profession and encouraged him in his efforts to improve it.

After four years in the peacetime army Upton was aware of many of its faults, but—with Emily's help—he did not despair. He started a movement to provide more reading matter, especially in military history, for officers stationed on the plains. Many of them, he felt, turned to drinking and gambling only as a way to pass the dull and lonely hours.[30] He spent long hours drilling his men and instilling discipline in them, telling Wilson that he had "always been at a loss how to explain the indifference of our celebrated generals during the war to these two essential elements of success." He hoped that his example would soon be adopted throughout the army.[31] His reform impulse was not limited to the army—he wrote his Congressman demanding a civil service bill.[32]

His happiness was short-lived. Emily found the hot Atlanta summer unhealthy, and in June she went to Willowbrook for the season. Her health failed to improve, and in November her doctor ordered her to Nassau. Still she showed no improvement, and by January Upton was receiving discouraging reports from her physician. In March, 1870, he learned that she was failing rapidly and he prepared to visit her in Nassau. Before he could even get out of Atlanta she died.

Her death was a blow, but he consoled himself with his faith. "She was prepared to go," Upton told his parents. "Her life was complete, and God has called her to Himself. I know that in her death I have been drawn nearer to Christ, and that I can now lay hold of the plan of salvation as I never could before." Most important, his certain faith in the resurrection of the body "robs death of its sting." He buried her near Willowbrook, and mourned her the rest of his life.[33]

Return to West Point

Upton hardly had time to formally mourn Emily. Just before she died, he heard rumors that President Grant had selected him as the next Commandant of Cadets at West Point, and soon after her death he received official appointment. On July 30, 1870, he returned to the familiar and secure grounds of West Point.[1]

As Commandant of Cadets, Upton was filling a post created by Sylvanus Thayer in 1825. He instructed the cadets in the duties of privates, noncommissioned officers, and officers, and in the tactics of the three arms of the service. He also took charge of the discipline and administration of the cadets. His only superior at the Academy was the Superintendent.

Upton spent the next five years at West Point. He was always busy, either with his duties, his reading, or making improvements in his tactics. His office was centrally located near the cadet barracks, and he was in it by 7:30 A.M. In the mornings he sat behind his desk and interviewed cadets who had been put on report the previous day. Upton required the boys to stand with heads uncovered and at attention while they stated the cause of their delinquencies. He then handed out punishment. In the afternoons he directed cadet drill. He soon came to know every boy at the Point, and was aware of most of the events going on there. He made it a rule to have all members of the First class to his quarters. His invitations were formal—"The Commandant of Cadets will be pleased to see Cadets London and Reed at tea this evening"—and so was the conversation.[2]

Soon after he arrived at the Academy, Upton discovered that upperclassmen were exacting pledges from members of the Fourth Class. Under pain of forfeiture of their furlough privileges, the plebes promised to forbear hazing the members of the following class. Upton objected to the practice on the grounds that right conduct should be based on higher motives. Superintendent Thomas G. Pitcher accepted his recommendation and abolished the pledges. Upton tried to raise the moral standards of the cadets in other ways. By his frequent attendance he encouraged their biweekly prayer meetings, and on Sundays he was always present at chapel.[3]

Close contact with the cadets was not always pleasant. Six months after he assumed his position as Commandant, Upton faced a serious problem. In 1871 New Year's day fell on a Sunday, so Superintendent Pitcher designated Monday, January 2, as a holiday. He allowed the First and Second Classes a dance and gave visiting privileges in barracks to the Third Class, but because the Fourth Class examinations were to begin the next day, he placed it under the customary restrictions. One Fourth Class cadet nevertheless decided to go to the neighboring village of Highland Falls. He arranged with his roommate to report that his absence, if discovered, was permissible and proper. Upton found out about his absence, heard the false report, learned of its falsity, and arrested both young men. He planned to bring charges against the offending cadets, order a trial before a general court-martial, and dismiss them if they were found guilty.

When members of the First Class learned of the incident they were indignant. The reputation of the Corps had recently been attacked on the grounds that the cadets were not as truthful as they had been before the war, so the First Class decided to set an example of the two Fourth Class cadets. At midnight of January 4 they forced the guilty boys to put on civilian clothes, took them outside the Academy grounds, gave them $50, and told them never to return. Neither Upton nor Pitcher knew of their actions until the next morning, when representatives of the First Class called on Upton and informed him of what they had done.

The seemingly childish actions taken by the First Class cadets were serious because the army prided itself on its discipline and functioned smoothly only when everyone in it followed the proper hierarchal channels. Further, West Point Honor System, which operated on the principle that a cadet's word was never questioned, was at stake. Upton could have arrested the ringleaders and dismissed them from the Academy for taking authority into their own hands, but he was so incensed with the Fourth Class cadets for having lied to him that he turned on them instead. As soon as he heard of what the First Class had done, Upton reported to Pitcher and sent an officer to bring the Fourth Class cadets back to the Academy. They returned on January 6. When Upton interviewed the cadets, he stated the nature of the charges against them for lying and the proof he had. They offered their resignations. Upton accepted them and sent the resignations on to Pitcher with a recommendation that, in order to avoid delay and useless mortification, the requisite parental consent be waived. Pitcher agreed. Meanwhile he issued an order in which he said that although the actions of the First Class were praiseworthy in motive he disapproved of their assumption of power. He assigned a light punishment to the class.

News of the incident spread, and on January 12 Congress voted to investigate. A committee of three Representatives soon arrived at West Point, spent one day asking questions,

and returned to Washington. It then issued a report cen-
suring Upton and Pitcher not only for failing to arrest the
leaders of the First Class but for recommending to the
guilty Fourth Class cadets that they resign. The committee
added that Upton and Pitcher gave a "virtual sanction to
the riotous proceedings of the class." Upton replied that the
First Class had been punished, that the Fourth Class cadets
would have been advised to resign in any event because of
the serious nature of their offense, and protested against
being "censured without a trial." He demanded a court of
inquiry.

To Wilson, Upton complained that "the false reports
circulated against the Academy are abominable. . . . Partisan
hatred is at the bottom of the whole thing." Upton thought
the committee, composed of two Republicans and one
Democrat, was trying to strike against President Grant, "no
matter how many molecules like Pitcher and myself suffer."

The Army refused to grant Upton a court of inquiry, and
a resolution introduced in Congress for that purpose failed
to pass. The Secretary of War relieved Pitcher later in the
year, appointing General Thomas H. Ruger in his place. In
June the two Fourth Class cadets returned to the Academy;
one graduated and the other flunked out.[4]

After the incident Upton returned to his routine. His sister
Sara kept house for him, and although he seldom engaged
in social activities, his professional duties kept him busy.
As he told Henry du Pont, "I wish very much to read and
improve my mind, but—West Point I find is not the place to
do it." [5] Upton thought Ruger a "model soldier" and boasted
that the Superintendent had put the Academy "on a splendid
footing." He was especially pleased when Ruger appointed
many young instructors to the faculty. "I can tell you with
all confidence," Upton reported to Du Pont, "that in the
future cadets must have some sense to graduate." [6]

There were other pleasant days for Upton. In February,

1873, the Secretary of War told Superintendent Ruger to bring the Corps of Cadets to Washington for the second inauguration of President Grant. He wanted to reward the cadets for their excellent behavior since the New Year's incident. Upton commanded the cadets at the ceremonies. For weeks the Commandant had the cadets busy repairing and polishing their uniforms and brass. On March 2 the Corps walked across the frozen Hudson River, caught the train, and arrived in Washington the next day. The city was filled with politicians, soldiers, diplomats, and a feeling of excitement. The cadets were the center of attention wherever they went, and the boys had a wonderful time seeing the city, staring at people, and being stared at in return.

At the inaugural the cadets gloried in their role as Grant's personal bodyguard. That night they attended the inaugural ball and supper, where they met and talked with some of the nation's leading statesmen. Anything that followed, it seemed, would be an anticlimax, but Upton had a special treat in store for them. On their last afternoon in Washington, Upton marched the cadets to General-in-chief Sherman's house. Sherman, Philip Sheridan, Oliver Otis Howard, Samuel P. Heintzelman, and other generals were inside, all in full dress uniform. As the cadets gasped, the generals walked out, greeted Upton, and inspected the Corps. Upton then had the cadets go through a dress parade. When they were finished Sherman ordered them to stack arms, then invited them inside for a reception. On their return home the cadets stopped in New York City and paraded up Broadway. The cadets were still dazed when they returned to West Point.[7]

Soon thereafter Sherman sent Upton an autographed copy of his recently published *Memoirs*. Upton read them, then told Sherman that "your contribution to history . . . will not only enhance your reputation but, what will be more gratifying to you, will attract the attention of Europe to the accomplishments of our arms, and open up a fertile field of illustrations to the future students of strategy and grand tactics." [8] Upton said the same things to Wilson and added that Sherman's book "shows him to be a great Captain." [9]

Sherman and Upton were developing a close relationship, based on their mutual respect and admiration—and on their mutual love for the army. Their official duties threw them together often, and when they were separated they corresponded frequently. Sherman, who was nineteen years older than Upton, treated him both as a protégé and a spokesman. The general-in-chief was an enthusiastic proponent of army and tactical reform, but he did not have time to devote to the details involved in those subjects. He came to rely upon Upton to articulate and later to supply his ideas. Before the war, Sherman's intellectual mentor had been Henry Halleck; after the conflict Upton, who was in many ways Halleck's successor as the army's chief theorician and advocate of reform, gradually took Halleck's place for Sherman. The general-in-chief was a man with a violent temper and strong prejudices. Upton shared most of his prejudices—especially those against civilians who meddled with the army. Further, Upton used Sherman as an aid to his advancement. The two officers had a beneficial relationship.

Sherman was always helpful. In 1869 the War Department appointed a board, headed by Generals John M. Schofield and Wesley Merritt, to assimilate Upton's infantry tactics to the artillery and cavalry. Upton was unhappy with their work, which he said was "full of errors." Further, he felt that the whole idea of assimilation was impractical and would "prove detrimental." [10] But, as other boards met and their results also failed to satisfy him, Upton realized that the War Department was determined to assimilate and so he decided to cooperate.[11] The Department's reasoning was sound; as Upton himself later pointed out, "The want of a system whereby the information and experience acquired in one arm of service may be made available in the others has long been felt in the Army." Both during and after the Civil War, artillery men had served as horse artillery, cavalry, and infantry, while the cavalry also served in all three arms. Uniform regulations would make transition easier.[12] After numerous conferences and correspondence with Sherman, Upton saw to the appointment of a new board, with himself at the head, to meet at West Point and assimilate the tactics of the three arms.[13]

The other members, whom Sherman allowed Upton to select, included Du Pont, an artillery expert, Colonel John Eaton Tourtellotte, a lawyer who had remained in the army after volunteer experience in the Civil War and who was Sherman's personal aide, and Captain Alfred E. Bates, an instructor in cavalry tactics at West Point.[14] Upton thought their task would be the easy one of adjusting the commands. He promised Du Pont that his duties as Commandant would not interfere with their work, and looked forward to devoting six to nine hours daily to assimilation.[15]

Upton and Du Pont had known each other since their own cadet days, when they were members of the same class. They merely tolerated each other then, however, because Du Pont was a moderate on the slavery question and Upton disapproved of his views. Moreover, their backgrounds were different. Upton was a poor boy from a rural home; Du Pont, scion of one of America's successful business families, was distinguished for his gracious, courtly manners. Upton felt no affinity for the sensitive, handsome Du Pont. But Du Pont had an excellent war record with the artillery, and he had remained with that arm after the conflict. Further, Du Pont was interested in tactical reform, and the two men were soon exchanging ideas. Upton fell into the habit of express-

ing his views to Du Pont as he had once expressed them to
Emily. Their service at West Point on the board brought
them closer together.

Du Pont and the other members of the board arrived at
the Academy in the middle of January, 1873, and immediately went to work. Du Pont reported to his parents that
they were laboring nine hours a day "in a business which
requires the closest attention." [16] In order to test the practical results of their assimilation as it progressed, Upton and
Du Pont taught the cadets the new drill systems. As cadets,
the two men had often complained because one of their
predecessors in tactical reform, Commandant William J.
Hardee, had used them to perform his experiments. Now it
was their turn, and Upton and Du Pont kept the cadets busy
learning new artillery and cavalry drills. [17]

By March Upton was satisfied with their progress. He was
especially pleased with the cavalry tactics. [18] Even Colonel
Tourtellotte, who had been the most pessimistic member
of the board, was becoming enthusiastic. [19] Meanwhile
Appleton and Company, Upton's publishers, had agreed to
publish the new works, and Bates and Upton spent nearly
a week posing for the plates illustrating the manual of arms.
Upton hoped everything would be finished by August. [20]

In June Upton had an interview with the Secretary of
War and the general-in-chief, both of whom were pleased
with the board's work. Three weeks later the War Department informed Upton, under injunctions of secrecy, that the
assimilated tactics of his board would be adopted by the
army. [21] But Du Pont had become engaged to a New York
woman, and whenever he could he left the Point to go to
the city. His frequent absences kept delaying the work, and
by August General Sherman was becoming impatient. Upton
assured Du Pont that he was "resolved not to be stampeded.
It is our reputation that is at stake, and the only safe course
is to make haste slowly." Even if the board finished its work,

Appleton and Company was having trouble with the plates, so the results could not be published for sometime. Whatever happened, Upton was confident, since "the fact is our work all around has had so many tests that we can't make any great mistakes." [22] Upton talked with Sherman, explained the cause of the delay, and got the General-in-chief to agree that a December publication would be satisfactory. Meanwhile Editor Church, in *The Army and Navy Journal*, expressed a hope that the new tactics would be finished in time for the spring drills.[23]

Upton's revised *Infantry Tactics* appeared in late 1873. He had made some minor changes from the earlier edition, especially in drill formations, to assure uniformity in the drill of the three arms. His basic ideas—the "fours," the heavy skirmish line, the light column—remained.[24] *Cavalry Tactics*, without a credit line, was ready for distribution in early 1874 and Du Pont's work, *Artillery Tactics*, appeared —also without a credit line—in 1875.[25] The published results pleased Upton. "All in all," he told Du Pont, "I think we ought to be proud. We have at least given a successful basis upon which to work." [26] He wished the government would grant some suitable recognition. "I fear however we shall have to find our reward in the satisfaction which results from contemplating our labors." Still, that would not be inconsiderable, for Upton added, "I firmly believe that the three books will stand many years." Under the new system, drill and tactics of the artillery and cavalry conformed to those of the infantry. The basic drill unit was four mounted men or four guns and the heavy skirmish line was the ordinary tactical formation.

Colonel Du Pont married as soon as the work was completed. He had always been torn between his social and business obligations as a member of the Du Pont family, and his desire to be a professional soldier; soon after his marriage he resigned from the army to work in the family firm and to become a railroad executive. Just before he married, Du Pont took time to send Upton a gift. Upton thanked him for the "statuettes," remarking that the gift would remind him of many hours of hard work together.[27]

One immediate problem facing Upton was a claim by Henry J. Hunt that a board of which he had been a member, in 1856, should receive credit for the artillery tactics. In reviewing *Artillery Tactics*, Hunt criticized it. He then wrote to both Sherman and Upton demanding compensation for the work of his board. Sherman defended the Upton board, praising its work as original, and Hunt dropped his claim.[28]

While he was working on the assimilation, Upton had told Church, "It is my belief that our system of tactics for the three arms will be found, on investigation, to be superior to anything existing in Europe." [29] When he sent Church a copy of the revised *Infantry Tactics*, Upton asked the editor to leave aside minor considerations and look closely at the facility for passing from double to single rank and at the method of deploying skirmishers by numbers. Because the battalion was right behind the skirmishers to feed their line, Upton felt his system "will be found superior to any method prescribed in Europe for deploying skirmishers." [30]

In *The Army and Navy Journal* Church enthusiastically greeted each volume as it appeared. He was pleased that the tactics were now uniform, and noted that although Europeans always kept the drills of the three arms separate, their practice was "opposed to the spirit of our institutions." Americans were not specialists, but men ready and able to do "anything and everything." Church was delighted with the skirmish drill, the deployment from column, and the deployment by numbers. He thought the system, now used by all three arms, both so simple and so excellent that "the only wonder is that this movement was not used long ago." [31]

But Church's fine words could not still the critics, and as he felt that the function of the *Journal* was to serve as an organ of expression, Church printed all letters as they came in. One officer, signing himself "Sadowa," thought any attempt at assimilation foolish. "Why not," he asked, "make all the services use the same weapons?" Besides, he had wasted enough time learning new drill systems. "After cramming through Scott, Hardee, Casey, and Upton, we hoped that all would join in the exclamation, *Ohe! Jam satis.*" [32] Another officer felt that the only conceivable way in which assimilation of cavalry and infantry tactics could work would be to have the men go about on all fours or the horses on their hind legs. He preferred the latter solution.[33]

Most of the criticism came from cavalry officers, and at one point even Church wavered. In 1874, after printing two long letters which claimed that Upton's system was destroying the cavalry's primary function—the final charge with the saber—Church declared that he agreed. Upton's system, he said, made the cavalry everything but cavalry. Mounted rifles, dragoons, or mounted infantry it might be, but "as the tactics now stand it would save the Government a good many dollars, and our so-called 'cavalry' much needless trouble, to have every saber used by an enlisted man turned into the arsenals." [34] Upton responded to the criticism by asking his old cavalry commander, Wilson, to write an essay "for European officers" on the role of cavalry in modern war. He wanted Wilson to emphasize its diversified functions— scouting for information, reconnaissances in force, foraging, raids, destruction of railroads, intercepting communications, fighting other cavalry, fighting infantry, either as cavalry or dismounted infantry, assaulting entrenchments, and carrying fortified cities.[35] Upton also explained his system more fully to Church. The point of the assimilation and of the new cavalry tactics, he said, "was to increase the offensive power of cavalry as cavalry." The breech-loader made the offensive charge with the *arme blanche* obsolete. As Upton saw it, cavalry could best serve by galloping around the flank of an enemy, dismounting, and opening a vicious fire. The Europeans were just beginning to understand this, and Upton was surprised that an American who had participated in the Civil War should not.[36]

The future would show that Upton's contention was correct. Although tradition-oriented officers, especially in the cavalry itself, did try to retain the old methods, the breech-loader and later the machine-gun made it impossible. The Civil War had brought on a revolution in tactics, one which Upton saw but others tried to ignore. Henceforth firepower, not the bayonet or the saber, would decide battles. And the army, despite frequent protests, was to retain Upton's system.[37]

Less important but more irksome problems plagued Upton. Many officers claimed credit for the idea of division into fours, and some threatened lawsuits if Upton did not share his copyright and royalties with them. Upton fell into the habit of referring such matters to Sherman, who always answered with blistering letters to the complaining officer. Sherman admitted that Upton had borrowed ideas from various sources, but took the position that Upton had "combined all the advantages, and . . . must be remunerated." [38]

There were large sums of money involved. Upton published his *Tactics* privately and, thanks to adoption by the army (and thus automatically by the various state militias), he enjoyed huge sales. All military men in the United States, professional and amateur, were required to know Upton's *Tactics*. Upton published three different editions during his lifetime, each supplanting the other.[39] Further, in 1870, Upton responded to a request from Appleton and Company and published *Tactics for Non-Military Bodies, Adapted to the Instruction of Political Associations, Police Forces, Fire Organizations, Masonic, Odd-Fellows, and Other Civic Societies*. The head of the Grand Army of the Republic, General John A. Logan, ordered all departmental

Cadet Emory Upton, U.S.M.A. Class of 1861. "He found the soldier's life irresistible."

Colonel Henry A. du Pont. Scion of the Delaware business family, Du Pont was Upton's closest friend and associated with him on the revision of the *Tactics*.

Emily Martin Upton. "He mourned her the rest of his life."

James Harrison Wilson. Upton said of his Civil War service under Wilson: "I would commute the rest of my life for just six months of such service."

James Abram Garfield. As chairman of the Senate Committee on Military Affairs, he did everything he could to institute Upton's reforms.

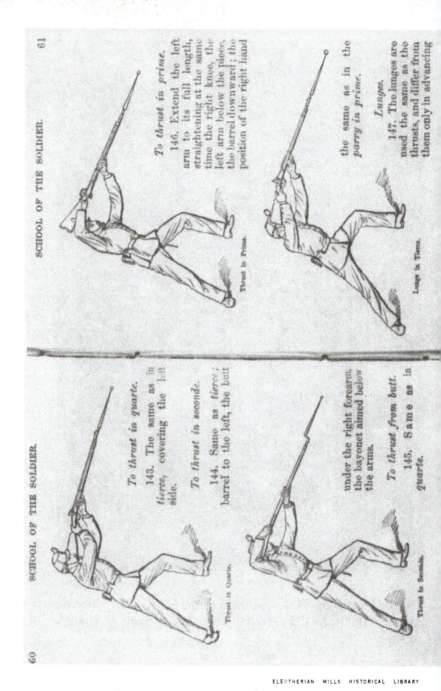

To thrust in prime.

146. Extend the left arm to its full length, straightening at the same time the right knee, the left arm below the piece, the barrel downward; the position of the right hand the same as in the *parry in prime.*

Lunges.

147. The lunges are used the same as the thrusts, and differ from them only in advancing

Thrust in Prime.

Lunge in Tierce.

To thrust in quarte.

143. The same as in tierce, covering the left side.

To thrust in seconde.

144. Same as tierce; barrel to the left, the butt under the right forearm, the bayonet aimed below the arms.

To thrust from butt.

145. Same as in quarte.

Thrust in Quarte.

Thrust in Seconde.

Plates from the revised *Tactics* published by D. Appleton and Company. Upton posed for the plates in June, 1873.

Right Shoulder Shift Arms.   No. 236.

William T. Sherman said of Emory Upton, "Thoughts are ephemeral. Deeds substantial. To unite both requires genius."

commanders of the GAR to adopt Upton's system for parades and public receptions. From the various editions Upton received a substantial royalty for the remainder of his life, sometimes amounting to more than $3,000 a year.[40] Coupled with his regular pay, the royalties made Upton financially comfortable.

Perhaps more pleasing, the Franco-Prussian War provided a good test of Upton's tactical ideas, and most of them held up well. The Germans and French found that the breech-loading rifle was startlingly effective in checking mass assaults and that the only realistic method of advance was by the leaps and bounds of small numbers of troops.[41]

In 1874, in a paper he delivered to the Thayer Club at the Academy, Upton analyzed Prussian tactics. The Prussians used the four-company-battalion, and ordinarily sent out two companies as skirmishers while keeping the other two, in separated columns, back. The advantages of the company column were great; the columns could be deployed in any direction; on the uneven ground over which much of the war was fought the column could adapt itself easier than a line; the column enabled the commander to keep his forces well in hand and allowed him to engage the minimum number of men required. Upton did have some objections to the Prussian system. He thought four companies to a battalion too few—the American army had ten—because the companies were cumbersome. Further, the Prussians did not have enough officers; each one-hundred-man American company had three officers, while the two-hundred-fifty-five man Prussian company had only five. Upton also thought that the German method of flowing around the flanks of strong points a mistake. It might work against the "inferior troops" of Austria or France, but if the Prussians tried it against the English or the Russians they would find their center pierced and their troops routed.

Upton's summary of the war was that "no new principles

in strategy or grand tactics have been established, and the only important change in minor tactics is the use of skirmishers to an extent heretofore unknown in Europe, but for which both parties would have been prepared if they had studied our civil war." [42]

The years following Emily's death had been profitable for Upton. He had worked hard enough to prevent despair over her death to turn to morbidity. Thirty-six years old in 1875, he had established a solid reputation for himself throughout the army. His name was known and respected by his fellow junior officers, his superiors, and the War Department. But the sense of frustration that had been with him since the end of the war remained. He was at the peak of his intellectual powers, and his ambitions were not satisfied. He began to look for new fortresses to storm, for a new Columbus to capture.

Redefining the Army's Role

Acting as an official observer for the United States Army, Upton spent the latter part of 1875 and most of 1876 on a world tour. He studied the major armies of the world, and he returned home filled with new ideas and a new purpose. In the last five years of his life Upton showed a single-minded devotion to that purpose, neglecting his tactics, his social life, and even the memory of his beloved Emily. The result was *The Armies of Asia and Europe* and *The Military Policy of the United States*, works which were both monuments to his research and clarion calls for army reform. Ultimately, Upton's writings had an important influence on American military doctrine, but during his lifetime Upton found himself, and his demands for army reform, ignored. Still, with Emily gone, there was nothing else to which he could dedicate himself, and so he continued his work with fatalistic perseverance.

As early as 1871 Upton, despite the opportunities his position at West Point gave him to experiment with tactical evolutions, felt bored and stifled. From the day he had entered Oberlin until the end of the Civil War, his career had been marked by rapid advancement. Now, after seven years of peace, he was still a lieutenant colonel. When his tour of duty at West Point was finished he could look forward only to unrewarding, arduous service on the plains. Upton began to feel that he was being left behind, shelved and forgotten. His tactical reform was complete, and the possibility of his bringing about significant reform in the broader area of the military structure of the nation seemed remote.

The post–Civil War American army was in the doldrums. Reduced in size by Congress until it numbered less than 25,000 officers and men, it had little to offer the ambitious soldier. Promotion was slow, opportunities for heroism few, and (except at West Point) intellectual activity absent. Line officers never even saw staff officers. The latter ignored the General-in-chief and reported directly to the Secretary of War, so that there was no central direction or control. Sherman complained that "so long as this is the case I surely do not command the Army of the United States, and am not responsible for it," and after an unsuccessful attempt to assert himself as head of the army, Sherman gave up in disgust and moved his headquarters to St. Louis.[1] When even the General-in-chief despaired of changing the basic organization of the army, Upton began to look for new fields in which he could apply his talents.

In the fall of 1871, former Secretary of State William H. Seward visited West Point; Upton took the opportunity of a long conversation with him to suggest that Seward use his connections to secure Upton a position with the Chinese army. Upton said that service with the Chinese would allow him to develop both his own talents and the military resources of a friendly nation. He asked for $150,000 as an immediate indemnity plus his usual annual salary. Seward, anxious to improve relations with China, talked with President Grant, who agreed to the proposal. Seward then asked the American minister in China to make the proposition to the Asian government. The minister replied that there was no Chinese army, but only a collection of provincial armies in which foreigners employed in instructing the troops in the art of war were treated as drill sergeants. He felt sure Upton did not want a position in China.

Rebuffed, Upton still was not ready to go with his regiment into the field and thus give up all possibility of effecting some reform somewhere. He turned to Sherman and proposed a world tour, which would allow him to recommend reforms in the American army on the basis of what he had seen in other armies. Sherman was enthusiastic and several times thought he had found the funds to send Upton, but something always interfered.[2] Upton was considering taking a year's leave of absence in order to study the European armies, even if at his own expense, when in 1875 Sherman finally induced Secretary of War William W. Belknap to have the War Department sponsor a tour.

On June 23, 1875, Upton received his orders. Belknap wanted him to travel through Asia and Europe, reporting on all the armies he observed. Upton should pay special attiontion to the Germans and their schools of instruction. In a covering letter, Sherman, on the other hand, emphasized that the Americans already knew enough of the armed forces of Western Europe, but nothing of those in Asia. He urged Upton to see what could be learned from them.[3]

As soon as final exams were over, Upton prepared to leave West Point. Major Joseph P. Sanger, an expert in artillery, and General George A. "Sandy" Forsyth, a cavalryman, joined him there. They would accompany him on the tour. By late June he was ready, and just found time to congratulate Du Pont on the birth of a daughter, his first child, before leaving West Point. In July, Upton and his companions traveled by train across the country. On August 2 they sailed from San Francisco for Japan where they spent a month. Upton was impressed with the Japanese efforts to enter the modern world, but disgusted with their pagan religion. From Japan, the delegation sailed to China, where it spent another month.

While in China, Upton tried once again to sell his services as a mental mercenary. He offered, on the same terms he had presented in 1871, to create a military academy for China. Upton was seeking honor and prestige, both of which were difficult to attain in the peacetime American army. He would not undertake the service at any price unless assured that he would receive the full cooperation of the Chinese. If guaranteed the independence he requested, Upton would give to China "ten of the best years of my life." He would direct an academy, based on the West Point model, for 300 or 400 English-speaking Chinese boys. In the first six years he would personally direct all instruction and discipline; during the remaining four years the graduates would take control. The Chinese would soon have a large body of Western-trained officers. The government, however, was not interested, and once again Upton's attempt to become a reformer on a worldwide basis failed.

After leaving China the officers went to India, where in two and one-half months they visited all the larger military stations in the valley of the Ganges, talked with British officers, and watched the Indian army on maneuvers. Throughout the East, the officers enjoyed courteous treatment, but they agreed that they hoped never to see any Asiatics again, "except it be the Japanese." [4]

From India the delegation traveled overland to Sevastopol and Constantinople, then north to Moscow. In the summer of 1876 it toured Europe, studying the armies of the major land powers and England.[5] Throughout the tour Upton maintained an active correspondence with friends in the United States, most of which consisted of detailed descriptions of the scenes he saw and the unusual meals he ate. Contact with other cultures strengthened his contempt for them and reinforced his own religious views. Japan, he claimed, was "steadily progressing toward stable and well-regulated government" and needed only conversion to Christianity to complete its march towards civilization. And the conversion was coming. "The fullness of time is approaching. Idols are falling down, superstitions are giving way, but the human heart endures, and must fix its affections on Him who gave His body as a ransom for all." In Rome, recently occupied by the Italians, he was happy to see that the Italian officers were "all bitter against the Pope and priesthood." The soldiers were not atheistic, but they were disgusted "at the dissolute lives of the priests." Protestantism was on the increase in Rome, where "time must work reform. There is too much intelligence to permit religion to be made a mockery of much longer."

But Utopia, he knew, had not yet arrived in America. Friends kept him informed of the recurrent scandals in Grant's administration, which he vigorously condemned. Grant, Upton declared, "cannot construe sympathy with approval of his conduct," although "it will certainly do him good to know that those upon whom he has bestowed so much kindness will not forsake him." America needed permanent reform, "not a wave of indignation that sweeps a few knaves from office, to be succeeded only by others." Upton proposed a new system, with life tenure for most elective offices and higher salaries to attract better men.[6]

But his interest in religion and domestic reform was secondary. Upton was a career officer, devoted to his duty, and most interested in the ideas and opinions of his fellow professional soldiers. What he learned from them sharpened his own previous prejudices while filling him with specific new ideas which he eagerly anticipated applying in the United States.

The professional officers Upton met in Europe regarded the German system as the peak of military efficiency. Everywhere they were trying to emulate it, because it had proven

itself in 1864, 1866, and 1870, and because it was the culmi-
nation of diverse developments in military affairs in nineteenth-century Europe. After the overthrow of Napoleon
and the creation of a stable system in Europe, the leaders of
the continental states, shocked by and afraid of the revolutionary fervor Napoleon inspired, raised and trained their
armies at least as much for the suppression of insurgents at
home as for fighting abroad. The essential quality required of
such armies was loyalty, not efficiency. For this purpose
small forces of long-serving regulars, led by an exclusive,
aristocratic officer-corps, were ideal. The difficulty was that
if any one European state accepted the risk of internal
revolt and reverted to the mass army, the rest would perforce
have to follow or suffer defeat. But the danger appeared
slight because it seemed impossible to create an effective
mass army, based on universal conscription and short-term
service, which would be politically reliable.

The solution to the dilemma came from Prussia. During
the Napoleonic wars the Prussians, like the rest of Europe,
had adopted the principle of the nation in arms, but as
Prussia was not rich and could not afford a large military
budget, she had done so at the least possible cost. The
device used to create a cheap mass army was the Landwehr,
a militia organization composed of the country's most able-
bodied men. The regular Prussian army remained small, but
Prussia could put large numbers in the field by mobilizing
the militia. The Landwehr, however, was not as amenable
to the king's discipline as the regular army, because the
Landwehr officers were prominent local bourgeois and usually liberals, so the king only dared to call the militia to the
colors in a war of national defense. Still, the king and leading statesmen of the nation wanted Prussia to play the role
of a great power; to do so they had to keep the Landwehr
active and thus prepared to fight. But an active militia meant

an armed bourgeois which the king and his ministers feared.

Between 1815 and 1860 Prussia could not arrive at a solution to her problem. Choosing the lesser of evils, the Prussian leaders kept the army below 200,000 in size, which kept it loyal (and in 1848 the regulars proved their worth), while they allowed the Landwehr to diminish in importance. The trouble was that Prussia no longer counted as a major power and had to accept the humiliation of Olmütz.

In 1858 General Albrecht von Roon sent a memorandum on military reorganization to the regent, soon to be King William I. Roon began by describing the dangerous state of international relations and the perils Prussia faced, then launched into an attack on the Landwehr. It was a "politically false" institution, because it no longer impressed foreign governments, and "militarily false" because it lacked proper discipline. He then proposed to give Prussia a large and reliable army by the simple expedients of creating a larger, more active reserve and giving control of the officer-corps of the Landwehr to regular army officers. Roon would eliminate all men from the Landwehr who had not spent three years with the colors and four years with the reserve. Because he shortened the period conscripts would spend with the regular army, Roon allowed the army to train more men without necessitating an increase in the size of the army or the budget. With a three- instead of a five-year-period of service, the turnover rate was faster and more men would pass into the reserve each year. Further, the men of the militia would be uniformly disciplined, thanks to their service with the regulars. Each Landwehr battalion would be connected to an active regiment; officers in the Landwehr would be elected by the officer body of the regular army regiment, not by the Landwehr men. Thus, although the Landwehr would still reflect all the various factions in Prussian society, the members would be well disciplined, and its leadership would represent only the views of the aristocratic regular officer-corps.°

Roon's proposals met violent opposition in the *Landtag*, where liberals defended the Landwehr as the bulwark of the people's liberty and as a militarily proven institution. After a long and complicated battle, the new Chancellor Otto von Bismarck was able to get most of Roon's proposals instituted. Roon now had his well-trained, well-disciplined army under the control of professional officers. The ordinary conscript, after spending three years with the colors, spent four years in the active reserve (where he served for two eight-week periods on active service and attended muster twice a year) and then served five years in the Landwehr (which involved participating in company drill biannually for a period of fourteen days). The Prussian reserve system made a reliable mass army available to the king whenever he decided to mobilize. With it, the Prussians rolled back the Danes, the Austrians, and the French, unified Germany, and imposed their military system on the new nation. They became the wonders of the military world. Professionals everywhere looked to them for guidance.[7]

More was involved in the Prussian victories than mere size, and Upton was at least as much interested in the Prussians' command structure as in their organization and recruitment policy. The German general staff, commanded by Chief of Staff Helmuth von Moltke, stood at the head of

---

° In Prussia, each regiment in the field had a depot where the reserve and Landwehr troops were consolidated and trained, and from which it could draw replacements, which made it possible for regiments to operate at full strength most of the time. Sherman was impressed with this system, and he complained that the "greatest mistake in our Civil War" was to create new regiments, in which state governors granted commissions and controlled promotion, rather than filling existing ones with the new recruits. Upton was to echo that complaint in his writings. William T. Sherman, *Memoirs* (New York, 1890), II 387–88.

the army. In peacetime the general staff collected information regarding the organization, tactics, and armament of foreign armies, prepared plans for possible wars, and arranged the details for the mobilization, movement, and concentration of troops upon the outbreak of war. It also controlled the educational system, which included a variety of postgraduate schools for the various arms.

The general staff first came into prominence midway in the Danish War, when Moltke distinguished himself in the operations around Düppel and Jutland. During the Austrian War, the king empowered Moltke to give orders directly to commanding officers, thus freeing him from even the nominal control the civilian minister of war had formerly exercised, and making Moltke the supreme army commander. Moltke retained his independence during the Franco-Prussian War, where his plans led to swift victory. In the new Germany that followed unification the general staff was free from civilian restraint.[8]

After 1871 the independence of the German army from the Imperial Parliament was practically complete. Two examples must suffice: Germany was divided into some twenty army corps districts, and all the troops in a district—regulars, reserve, and Landwehr—belonged to that corps. The general commanding the corps had, in all military matters, absolute authority—he was independent of the Ministry of War and responsible to the emperor. And, thanks to Bismarck's "iron budget," the Prussian army was financially independent. In 1867 Bismarck induced Parliament to fix the size of the peacetime army at one per cent of the total population, with an allowance of 225 thalers per man for the next ten years. After the unification of Germany in 1871, the Imperial *Reichstag* renewed the arrangement for a three-year period. And in 1874 the arrangement was again made, this time for a seven-year period. Thus the army, and its budget, continually expanded. Throughout the rest of Western Europe and in the United States, career officers, who had their powers hedged in by numerous restraints erected by the bourgeois liberals who distrusted and feared the standing armies, regarded the German as fortunate. * Upton, who suffered each year as Congress cut the United States Army budget, was no exception.[9]

Upton traveled in Europe at a time when the Prussian system, as imposed upon Germany, was receiving the highest of all compliments—imitation. Greeks, Rumanians, Turks, and others, as well as Americans, trekked to Berlin to study. Meanwhile the French were copying their conquerors. Before 1870 the French had concentrated on creating a loyal, rather than a mass, army. Within the framework of universal conscription they built up a small army of long-term professionals. They selected by ballot, out of the age group liable, the number of men necessary to keep the army up to the size fixed by the legislature. Most men escaped conscription; those who did not served with the colors for seven years. When their term was up, it was too late for the conscripts to learn a trade, and they usually re-enlisted. The system satisfied both the preference of the officers for expert over amateur soldiers and of the bourgeois to escape service (bourgeois Frenchmen who drew a *Mauvais numéro* could purchase a substitute). Rejecting the Napoleonic tradition and the current Prussian practice, the French maintained that "the society in which everyone is a soldier

---

* Non-German soldiers were also jealous of the esteem in which the German people held their officers. Through his successes, Moltke destroyed the earlier bourgeois ideas about the incompetency of the soldier, even in military affairs; in fact, the Germans began to think of the officers as experts not only in war but other affairs, and elected Moltke and fellow officers to parliament. Alfred Vagts, *A History of Militarism: Civilian and Military* (rev. ed.; New York, 1959), 203. At the same time, the attitude in other countries towards the professional soldiers was well expressed by Gilbert and Sullivan in their "I am the very model of a modern major-general."

is a barbaric society." And, continued the speaker, the French statesman and historian Louis Adolphe Thiers, "in the countries where everyone is a soldier, everyone is a bad soldier . . . . Without specialization, no army at all." * The French were convinced that the efficiency of their 300,000 would more than compensate for Moltke's numbers (a half-million or more), but they were soon to learn that thanks to Roon the Prussians had a system which gave them both efficiency and numbers.[10]

The Franco-Prussian War destroyed some of the illusions of the old military men, both inside and outside of France. No longer could they believe that genius, dash, and discipline would suffice to defeat the mass army. The French learned the lesson well, and the new requblic which emerged from the conflict slavishly copied the Germans.

So did everyone else. In Italy, Austria, and to a certain extent even Russia, short-term active service for large numbers—with everyone spending a long period in the reserves —and variations on the general staff made their appearance. In England, Prime Minister William E. Gladstone directed Edward Cardwell to reform the army. Cardwell raised the educational requirements for officers, abolished the system of selling commissions, shortened the term of active service and increased the term in the reserve. He also started a move towards the creation of a general staff. In short, Cardwell turned the standing army from "a costly receptacle for veterans" into a "manufactory for making soldiers." In one respect Cardwell did swim against the stream—he provided for the complete supremacy of the Secretary for War and the War Office over the commander in chief and the army. British officers complained ("War cannot be carried on un-less full and undivided authority is given to the general

---

* French officers ignored the reply of the Left: "Thus to die for the rich would be the specialty of the poor."

entrusted by the Government with the conduct of the
military operations," one said), but Parliament would not
budge.[11]

Although Upton had participated in the greatest war of
the century—a war which, unlike Moltke, he was wise
enough not to dismiss as a contest between two armed
mobs—he nevertheless was impressed by the Prussian
achievements. Like his fellow non-German officers, Upton
regarded the Prussian system, with its general staff, mass
army, and freedom from civilian control, an ideal one. For
the remainder of his life, Upton was to attempt to get the
United States Congress to adopt army reforms based on the
Prussian model.

While on tour, Upton decided to do more than just report
on the armies he had observed. He would use his report
as a vehicle for advancing reform. This soon became his
primary consideration. In June, 1876, he wrote from Geneva
that "since arriving in Europe, I have discovered that our
military organization is so worthless that now I feel that
even a thousand pages would not suffice to show it up."
Four months later, from Germany, he declared, "I shall
devote most of my attention to . . . showing our reckless
extravagance in making war."

In the fall of 1876 Upton returned to the United States.
Sherman was able to get him a temporary assignment in
Washington so that he could work on his report. In February,
1877, he took a leave and went to Ringgold Barracks, on the
Rio Grande, to visit his sister, who had married General
Andrew J. Alexander, "and to make the acquaintance of
Upton Alexander, a very promising nephew." In March,
1877, he received a new assignment—superintendent of the
studies of the officers at the Artillery School of Practice at
Fortress Monroe, America's only postgraduate military
school.

Upton was the head of the faculty and had charge of a new course on strategy and grand tactics. As teacher of the course, he told Du Pont, "I hope to repay the government all of the expense it incurred in sending me abroad." He was enthusiastic about his post, for although he considered West Point "far superior" to any European academy for preparatory training, he felt that America had nothing to compare with the war colleges of the Europeans. Consequently most American generals were "ignorant . . . of all the principles of generalship." This would be corrected at Fortress Monroe, where Upton planned to "form a corps of officers who, in any future contest may be the chief reliance of the Government."

The next few months were busy ones. Upton got to know his fellow faculty members, prepared his new course, and continued to write his report. He told Du Pont that he had even less free time now than when revising the tactics, and that his report "so engrosses my attention that to go away for a day is impossible."

As he completed each chapter, Upton sent it to Du Pont, who served as his chief critic, usually helping to improve Upton's style. The conclusions, Upton told Du Pont, would shock many people, "as I intend to expose the vices of our systems, instead of simply describing the organizations abroad." Upton admitted that America could not "Germanize," but he firmly belived that "we can apply the principles of common sense." [12]

Upton originally intended to attach an historical analysis of American military policy to his report, but Sherman, after he read Upton's chapter on the Mexican War, advised against it. Sherman pointed out that since Upton attacked Congress in the chapter he was on delicate ground. Congress paid for Upton's European trip so that he could report on his observations, not so that he could attack the government. Upton accepted Sherman's advice and decided to make his history a separate monograph and to include in his report only his recommendations for reform. Historical justification could come later.[13] By December, Upton had finished the report, and asked Sherman to obtain funds from the War Department for its publication. Sherman was unable to get the money. Upton, determined to have his views presented to the public, contracted with his old publishers, D. Appleton and Company, and financed the publication at an eventual loss of nearly $1,000 to himself.[14]

In *The Armies of Asia and Europe* Upton ignored Sherman's suggestion that he see what Americans could learn from the Asians. Instead, Upton praised the Orientals when they imitated the West and damned them when they did not. The Chinese were "backward" because they neglected to hire European military advisers; the Japanese were slightly better, as they tried to learn from the Europeans and had sent observers to America; the Indian army, run by the British, was the best of a poor lot.

In his brief discussion of the Eastern armies, Upton made two major points, both of which foreshadowed subsequent recommendations for American policy. The Chinese army, he maintained, was weak because of its division into district or provincial forces, which made unified command, instruction, and action impossible. Japan's major failing was the lack of individuality among the troops, which "recent modifications in tactics require." [15]

Turning from Asia to Europe, Upton noted a paradox. The Occidentals, who claimed a higher civilization, took nearly eight million young men from their families and work to create armies whose object was less the preservation of internal order than it was to contend for new territory and increased power. The European system, he declared, exhausted national resources and taxed the ingenuity of statesmen to the utmost to maintain the huge armies.[16]

Upton refrained from making an editorial comment on the

paradox; the bulk of his work consisted of a description of the armies of Europe. He covered their organization, recruiting, discipline, schooling, and tactics, provided extensive statistics on the size of the armies in peace and war, and analysed the various general staffs. The book was technically excellent; a modern authority has said Upton's work "is a valuable mirror of the state of the military profession" in the second half of the nineteenth century.

In his last chapter, Upton enumerated the general principles common to all European armies. Europeans considered it axiomatic that all citizens owed military service to their nation. The next basic assumption was that the regular army existed as the sole offensive and chief defensive agency of the state, and that it drew its strength from and was responsible to the central government. All armies operated on two footings, peace and war. The purpose of the peacetime army was to train officers and men for war. To accomplish that aim, men spent three to five years with the colors, then nine to fifteen years with the reserves. To retain continuity and insure competency, regular army officers elected the officers of the reserves. In the regular army itself, no man received a commission unless he had graduated from a military school or had passed a special examination. War academies educated officers in the art of war and prepared them for high command. To prevent stagnation officers passed constantly from staff to line and back again. A section of the general staff kept complete personnel records on every officer to enable the armies to profit from their best talent. Rapid, linear promotion, based on zeal and professional ability, encouraged young officers to work harder. To simplify administration and build up morale, the armies divided each nation into military districts with permanently assigned army corps, divisions, brigades, regiments, and battalions. Each conscript always served with the same unit, and each regiment had its own depot from which, in wartime, trained reserves went

forward as needed. This assured divisional and corps commanders that their regiments were always operating at full
strength. Finally the general staffs provided a central agency,
free from civilian control, for directing the armies. Not one
of these principles, all of which European soldiers considered
essential to the maintenance of an efficient army, had been
accepted in the United States.[17]

The application of these principles by Prussia in 1866
enabled her to defeat Austria in six weeks; in 1870 it took
her only three and a half months to destroy the French
army. And because Prussia was prepared for war it won with
small losses in men and material. By contrast, American
policy resulted in long, expensive wars marked by unnecessary losses in men, material, and money.

Cost would continue to be one of Upton's major themes.
Throughout the Western world opponents of army reform
usually centered their attack around the increased financial
burden the new armies would necessitate. Upton met the
argument by claiming that although an expansive army cost
more in peacetime it saved huge sums in war by making
quick, easy victories possible. The American system was one
of "false economy"; thirteen years after the Civil War the
country was still paying an annual sum of $1,150,000 in
interest alone on the war debt. If that much had been spent
for just two years before the war, the North could have
finished its task at Bull Run. Moreover in the long run the
Prussians, thanks to their preparedness, needed fewer troops
to accomplish more than the Americans. Judged by the
balance sheet, the well-organized, expansive army was
superior to the current American practice.[18]

Time and again Upton would refer to the ease of the
Prussian victories, always giving credit to their preparedness.
He never grappled with the problem of what would happen
when both sides were prepared, as they were in 1914; he
assumed that preparedness always led to quick, cheap vic-

tories. But he was not alone—most European soldiers in 1914 expected a short war.

Although Upton realized that America's problem was different from that of Prussia, he believed that the broad outlines of Roon's system could also meet America's needs. Upton knew that he need not worry about the loyalty of American troops. His task was to overcome both the opposition to spending more money on an army which most politicians thought was already doing a satisfactory job and to meet the prejudice which glorified the minuteman tradition. Operating from within the framework built by Roon, Upton proposed two alternatives. The United States could either so organize the regular army that "by the mere process of filling its cadres, it may be expanded to such proportions as to enable it, without other aid, to bring our wars to a speedy conclusion," or it could prosecute future wars with volunteer infantry, leaving the artillery and cavalry in the hands of the regulars. Under the second plan, the regulars would supply the bulk of the officers for the volunteer infantry.

Either plan would accomplish the same end—the regular army, rather than being organized as a completed entity capable only of fighting Indians, would provide a cadre for the armed forces of the nation in time of war. All troops would serve under trained officers, most of whom would come from the regular army.

In Upton's scheme the regular army need not number more than 25,000 men. The basic organizational unit would be the battalion, two for each regiment. However, regiments would contain enough officers for three or four battalions. In an emergency mobilization the reserves—whom Upton called the "National Volunteers" in order to satisfy the public's prejudice for volunteers—would fill the two skeleton battalions. Companies would also organize on the expansive principle. In peace a company would include three officers and fifty-four men, while in war the numbers would be increased to five officers and two hundred forty-two men. Thus the army could be doubled or tripled overnight. The extra officers would be obtained from noncommissioned officers who had passed a special examination, graduates of the course in military affairs offered to land-grant colleges, graduates of the various private military academies, or officers of the militia who could pass a special examination. In any case no unqualified man—no matter how powerful politically—would command in war. Upton also proposed that the United States follow the Prussian lead and establish depots, where replacements could be gathered, trained, and eventually sent forward to regiments at the front as needed.[19]

In his own way, Upton was trying to meet the traditions of America. Although he claimed that he was presenting the best possible system "to meet the demands of judicious economy in peace, and to avert unnecessary extravagance, disaster, and bloodshed, in time of war," he dared not go too far in copying the Europeans. He never advocated a peacetime conscription or short-term service with the colors, and his "National Volunteers" did not constitute a true reserve, because the troops would receive no training in peacetime— they were merely men who would volunteer to serve under regular army personnel in an emergency. But on his key proposal—that the armed forces of the nation should be led and controlled by the regular army—he never wavered.

Upton knew that before his reforms could be adopted the public would have to accept certain basic principles. He asked for a declaration that every able-bodied male citizen owed military service, a concept "thoroughly republican in its nature," because it put all classes in the same category. This came close to advocating universal conscription, which Upton had previously said he did not want, but which in fact he admired but never dared advocate. He did declare that the pernicious bounty and substitute systems had to be abandoned, once and for all. Americans had to realize that the power to grant a commission was the exclusive right of the President and must be taken away from the state governors. Most important, the country had to acknowledge that, by the very nature of the thing, the defense of the nation rested with the regular army, not the state militia units. America could no longer afford to muddle along relying on the minuteman tradition.

To meet its responsibilities, the army itself needed reforming. It had to abandon the current staff system (the so-called American general staff was composed of the heads of the various bureaus and departments and never met together for planning or direction), and through the consolidation of the Adjutant General's and Inspector General's Departments, create a true general staff. The first two sections of the new staff, under the command of the Secretary of War, would handle the army's paper work. In addition there should be three other sections, responsible to the General-in-chief. The first would collect information relating to all foreign armies; the second would study and write the history of American wars; the third would maintain an individual history of each officer in the army. The personnel of all sections should be encouraged to study the art of war. Thus most staff officers would be relieved of the burdensome routine of paper work and could concentrate on their real duties.

Perhaps because of his friendship with Sherman, Upton ignored the position of the General-in-chief in his recommendations. He made no clear, unequivocal call for eliminating the post (it was unknown in the Prussian Army), although if a true general staff were created with a chief of staff who would become supreme commander in wartime to head it, the General-in-chief was doomed. By neglecting the problem, Upton contributed to the later confusion which characterized the first attempts to create a general staff in America, and made possible the struggle over authority between John J. Pershing, Commander in Chief of the American Expeditionary Forces in 1917–18, and Peyton C. March, the chief of staff.[20]

Upton was more logical in his other demands. To complement the general staff, he urged the creation of a broader program of postgraduate military education, calling for an infantry school at Atlanta, a cavalry school at Fortress Monroe, and a War College to cap the entire system.[21]

One of his major demands was for constant interchange from the staff to the line. The advantages of such a policy would be great; the staff could find and use the highest talent and skill in the army; staff officers would not become slaves to routine, but rather they would become cognizant of the needs and wants of the troops; service on every level would eventually qualify officers for the higher grades; the army would profit by the periodic return of talented staff officers to the line. Operating under a system of alternate duty, European staff officers aimed only to qualify themselves for duty in battle, while American staff officers, with no prospect of commanding in action, became immersed in the drudgery of official routine.[22] Upton also asked the government to give company commanders greater disciplinary powers, to institute a system of compulsory retirement, and to base promotion on ability and not seniority. Moreover, he wanted all recruiting under the control of the regular army, which should divide the nation into military districts and subdistricts, each with its own regimental depot.[23]

The suggestions blended Upton's drive to reform and his ambition. Nearly every one of his reforms, if adopted, would have an immediate beneficial effect upon him. A staff appointment would give him an immediate promotion; a system of advancement based on ability and not seniority would be a boon to a young lieutenant colonel. But, as he had done before and would again, Upton convinced himself that his motives were for the good of the army. The best men in the army, he knew, had resigned because advancement came only to the mediocre who had the perseverance to wait their turn for promotion. He saw himself as an outstanding example of talent being ignored or passed over. The army therefore must reform itself so that men like himself would get ahead, else every man with talent would resign.

But only on the last page of *The Armies of Asia and Europe* did Upton face his major problem—the lack of any obvious danger which could justify a major and expensive reform in an army which was doing its job, Indian fighting, well enough to satisfy most Americans. He touched on the threat the Canadians, the Mexicans, and the Spanish in Cuba posed but, knowing that most politicians would not be impressed, he fell back on the menace of labor radicals. Numerous strikes and riots, which the militia had been incapable of controlling, marked the summer of 1877. Upton maintained that a few battalions of national volunteers, commanded by regular army officers, would have sufficed to prevent the bloodshed and loss of property.[24]

By arguing that Congress take the necessary steps to create a professional army in the United States in order to crush striking workers, Upton was making an almost abject confession of failure. Even in Europe, where large segments of the population were opposed to the system under which they lived and would have overthrown it if they could, the armies no longer existed for purposes of internal security. In America, where the great bulk of the people supported the system, the army could never fall back on internal security as a justification for its existence. Although Upton joined the politicians in emphasizing the "danger to our institutions" inherent in the rise of organized labor, he did not believe it himself and did not expect others to.[25]

Upton could only justify his system with reference to the future. A combination of developments in the late sixties and seventies, both in Europe and the new world, foreshadowed the end of American isolation and dictated a need for a new definition of the army's role. The fantastic speed of the industrial revolution was shrinking distances while making possible mass armies (thanks to better communications, which allowed generals to control more troops, and the ability of industry to supply more of the tools of war) at a time when growing nationalism and imperialism created dangerous tensions. Simultaneously, rapid industrialization made possible big navies, which would allow European powers to bring their mass armies to the new world. Like Alfred Thayer Mahan in the Navy, Upton saw and feared the possibilities of the emerging modern world, and he wanted America to be ready to meet them.[26]

Concurrently, the disappearance of the frontier and the Indian menace was depriving the army of its traditional function. Upton knew that the American army was never ready for major war because, since the days of George Washington, the government had maintained the army for the one job of Indian fighting. Unlike European armies, the American army had been engaged in almost continuous conflict for over a century. This was the major factor in its failure to develop a general staff—there was no time to plan for future developments in an agency whose function was a current and immediate one. But, by the late seventies, the army had mastered the Indians.* Congress recognized that

---

* In 1874 the House Committee on Military Affairs declared that the troops in the Department of the Lakes and on the Atlantic and Pacific seaboards, numbering 5,000, gave the United States an adequate reserve. These troops were currently of little use "as the policy of reconciling and pacifying the Indians progresses to a successful completion. Besides these there is a large number of troops stationed in the interior, having no special duty to perform." Reduction in the size of the army was therefore safe. C. Joseph Bernardo and Eugene H. Bacon, *American Military Policy: Its Development Since 1775* (2nd ed.; Harrisburg, 1961), 239.

fact when it reduced the size of the army from 50,000 in 1865 to 30,000 in 1870 and then, in 1874, to 25,000. As early as the 1840's, Henry Halleck had warned that the army's Indian fighting role was transitory, and that the army needed a more permanent function or it would soon have no *raison d'être*. Upton was seeing the fulfillment of Halleck's prophecy.[27]

Looking into the void (with the Indians gone, there was no logical limit to the length Congress could go in reducing the army), and to America's future in the modern world, Upton proposed to redefine the army's functions. The army, he felt, should be the sole agency responsible for national defense. It could meet that responsibility if the nation would adopt the National Volunteers program. This system, Upton maintained, was one which would give the United States a minimal defense force, in case of European aggression, at a minimal cost. He estimated that the expense of instituting his reforms would not run over $15,000,000. He never advocated a larger regular army, much less a large standing army or peacetime conscription. He was only trying to find "some method whereby both in peace and war we may have a national force ready to increase, and support, our troops in the field." He claimed to be content to see the regular forces remain at around 25,000, but as long as the country was going to maintain an army, it might as well be one prepared to do something.*

---

* Ever since the publication of *The Armies of Asia and Europe*, critics have maintained that Upton was a "big army man," which rubbed against the American grain at a time when there was absolutely no reason for increasing the size of the army. They pointed out that his 140,000 national volunteers were insufficient to wage modern war, and for purposes of internal security the national volunteers were superfluous. In two ways these criticisms, available in the letters printed in the *Army and Navy Journal* for the latter half of 1878, miss the point. Upton was not primarily a "big army man,"

Upton knew that his system could not bring America up to the standards of the Europeans, but that was not immediately necessary anyway. What he wanted was a public acceptance of the principle that only the regular army—and not civilians in arms—was capable of defending the nation. Once that principle had been accepted, then the regular army would naturally and logically grow—otherwise it could not meet its responsibility for national defense. Upton did not need to ask for a larger army—that would be the result of the acceptance of the earlier part of his program.

It was a revolutionary program. Although the National Volunteers did pay obeisance to the minuteman tradition, Upton was attempting to destroy the state militia and the state-controlled volunteer units while drastically changing the nature of the army's role and of its power. He tried to disguise his basic aim by claiming that the National Volunteers "would differ only from the volunteer regiments of the Civil War in having at the beginning trained officers to lead every company," but he knew that much more was involved.[28]

Upton was trying to do for America what Roon had done for Germany—find an adequate reserve system to support a strong, reliable, and proficient regular army. The Civil War had shown that the old militia system was a failure, and in the next war the country would not have time to train volunteers during the conflict. But the problem Upton raised was not faced until the twentieth century.

Upton's system would have given America a new, professional army, controlled by the national government. He

his national volunteers were intended to be merely the entering wedge in getting the American public to accept the principle of regular army responsibility for national defense. A "big army" would probably result, and Upton would not oppose it, but this was not his main objective.

consistently denounced every effort on the part of state authorities to retain any control over the armed forces of the nation. For the next two years he would do research in American military history in an attempt to prove that it was disastrous to allow a division in the armed might of the nation, with one force for Indian fighting and another, un-organized and lacking in central control and efficient leader-ship, for major conflicts.

In the last analysis, in asking for the elimination of the state militia and the amateur commanders who obtained their commissions through political rather than military skill, Upton may have been placing himself in opposition to the American tradition, but he was only doing so along with most of the rest of the nation. Nineteenth-century Americans still paid their respects to the jack-of-all-trades heritage but, like the other peoples of the Western world, they lived and gloried in an age of specialization. Doctors, lawyers, teachers, and mechanics were all creating their own organizations and erecting educational requirements before allowing an outsider to practice their trade. Upton wanted the same respect paid to specialized knowledge in the mili-tary field. He agreed with Halleck, who had complained before the Civil War, "It requires a professional man to conduct a law suit where a few thousand dollars are in-volved; but *mere* politicians can conduct armies where thousands of human lives, millions of money and the safety of the Government itself are involved."[29]

Upton and Halleck were more in accord with the mood of the nineteenth century than the great champion of the volun-teer civilian army, General John A. Logan. An Illinois politician and volunteer soldier himself, General Logan de-voted his later life to denouncing the professional soldier and glorifying the volunteer. His arguments were tinged with Jacksonian suspicion of the expert, and his final contention, that military genius was inherent and could not be taught, was more in conflict with the age than the ideas of Halleck and Upton.[30]

What Upton failed to realize was that although Americans accepted specialization in matters clearly involving technical skills, they still regarded politics and military policy in its largest sense as nontechnical. Logan was wrong in supposing that the specialized functions of the army could be handled by civilian volunteers, but so was Upton in feeling that *all* question of military policy should be controlled by the army. Upton's system would not be approved by the American people, who would not give complete control of the armed forces of the nation to the regular army. Upton's system did not succeed because it was rooted in the German, not the American, experience. Rather than study American society and then fashion military institutions within its framework, Upton worked from fixed views of military policy and then despaired because he could not shape the nation in accordance with their demands.[31]

Army men received *The Armies of Asia and Europe* enthusiastically.° Upton was pleased with and encouraged by the "friendly" reviews.[32] Church ran a series of editorials in *The Army and Navy Journal* praising it. Congress created a committee to investigate the need for a reorganization of the staff system with a West Point graduate, Ambrose Burnside, as chairman. In the states, after the disastrous failure of the

---

° The British soldier-historian, Lieutenant General Sir John Winthrop Hackett, has pointed out that "the years between 1860 and World War I saw the emergence of a distinctive American professional military ethic, with the American officer regarding himself as a member no longer of a fighting profession only, to which anybody might belong, but as a member of a learned profession whose students are students for life." Upton was more responsible for this development than anyone else in the army. John W. Hackett, *The Profession of Arms* (London, 1962), 38.

militia in the summer of 1877, politicians publicly wondered if it were not time to do something to reform the militia.[33] Upton could look forward to the future with confidence. Army reform was in the air and, thanks to the reputation he had established with the publication of his report, Upton could expect to be called upon as an expert advisor. He could even dare hope that the American army was about to emerge from the doldrums and that it might become a force organized to fight war with major powers rather than Indians. If it did, he knew much of the credit would belong to him.

The Military Policy
of the United States

While Upton was trying to redefine the army's role, the army was losing prestige. It was unseen, unpopular, or unknown. Northerners were disinterested in it, southerners disliked it, westerners no longer needed it. In 1877, as a result of political manipulations centering around the end of Reconstruction, the officers and men of the United States Army went a full year without pay. Officers despaired of promotion— many held the same rank for twenty or thirty years. They had no opportunity to advance their professional knowledge. Congress limited the size of the army to 25,000 men, and even then not enough recruits could be found to fill its ranks. Few respectable men would enlist—recruits were derelicts or illiterate immigrants. It was difficult to get more than one company together. At the posts on the frontier and, to a lesser extent, on the Eastern seaboard, the soldier's main problem was to overcome an endless boredom. Only an occasional parade drill broke the routine. The army's dark ages had descended.[1]

In an attempt to stimulate a renaissance Upton tried to popularize some of the ideas he had expressed in *The Armies of Asia and Europe*. In February, 1877, he published an article in *The Army and Navy Journal* advocating an expansive army, interchangeable service between the staff and line, territorial recruitment districts, and a war college. There was nothing new in what he said, but the *Journal* reached a wider audience than the *Armies of Asia and Europe* had. In an editorial Church praised Upton's proposals.[2] In March, 1878, in the *Journal,* Upton analyzed the causes of the failure of the American militia. The first great mistake, he claimed, was in neglecting to enforce the provision in the law which made every able-bodied man from eighteen to forty-five liable to service. The second was in presupposing that there was danger to popular liberty in a standing army. "The Army has proved, as we all know, the conservator of law and liberty, of property and life, instead of the destroyer of them." Upton maintained that there was no point in attempting to strengthen or reform the militia, because it would be cheaper and more efficient to improve the regular army.

Upton was not the only one concerned with the nation's defenses. In 1879 an anonymous writer in the *Atlantic Monthly* seconded Upton's conclusions about the militia. He said that the proper policy for the United States was to do away with the militia and substitute for it a force of national volunteers. They should be organized by the War Department and commanded by the President. The country should strengthen the regular army in order to furnish instructors to the volunteers and establish a system of popular instruction in the elements of military art and science in the colleges.[3]

In order to encourage more reform activity Upton, throughout his tour at Fortress Monroe, kept up an active correspondence with army officers. His purpose was to instill in them some of his enthusiasm for remaking the army and to create support for his own specific proposals. In April, 1878, he asked Wilson—now a prominent railroad director— to write an article on the importance and necessity of establishing depots. Upton wanted permanent depots for each regiment, where recruits would be inducted and trained and from which they could be sent forward as needed. His aim was to make certain that in time of war each regiment operated at full strength. He wanted one depot in each Congressional district, which he felt would enlist business support.[4]

Others were interested in reforming and raising the prestige of the army. James A. Garfield, major general in the volunteer army during the Civil War and Republican representative from Ohio, long had been a friend of the regular army. In 1866, speaking against a compulsory retirement bill, he declared, "Our present Army has in it more history, more glory and the record of more heroism and patriotism than any other army that ever existed."[5] In 1869, as a member of the House Committee of Military Affairs, he offered a bill to reduce the staff corps of the army and to bring it under the control of the General-in-chief. The staff officers, rather than acknowledging the General-in-chief as the head of the army, chose to magnify the duties of the Secretary of War and look to him as their sole and legitimate superior. As the Secretary was seldom well enough versed in military affairs to dominate them they thus made themselves virtually independent. The results were chaotic. The Ordnance Department, for example, supplied the guns which the Engineers mounted on the fortifications. The resulting emplacement was then turned over to the line without either the General-in-chief or the line officers who would man it being able to make the slightest suggestion. The General-in-chief, limited to a small personal staff, had no effective means of either commanding the army or planning for possible military campaigns. But although the Secretary of War, John Schofield, agreed with Garfield that the staff should report to the General-in-chief and not to the Secretary, the Washington-based officers, desiring to retain their independence, lobbied effectively and succeeded in getting Garfield's bill laid on the table.[6]

Garfield continued to push. In 1872 his committee called for hearings on army-staff organization. Upton was one of the officers called to testify. Although he used the hearing to advance his general reforms, for the most part he stuck to the point, which was control of staff bureaus. Every non-staff officer who testified, including Upton, thought the staff should be made to report to the General-in-chief, not to the Secretary of War. Again, however, the staff officers blocked action.[7]

In June of 1878 Garfield helped set up a joint committee "to study and report on the establishment of a sound military system for the United States." The chairman was Ambrose Burnside (now a Senator), and the other two Senators and four Representatives were all officers with experience in the Civil War. On July 22, in White Sulphur Springs, West Virginia, the hearing began. Sherman was the first witness. He denounced the militia and supported his position with George Washington's writings—writings which Upton had provided for the General-in-chief. Sherman also referred the committee to *The Armies of Asia and Europe,* and informed it of Upton's current project, a study of the military policy of the United States. The work, Sherman said, "will contain much valuable matter bearing on all the questions submitted to you."

As in earlier hearings on army reorganization, officers of the line condemned the independent staff bureaus. General John Pope thought the Secretary of War too powerful, argued that the staff officers should report to the General-in-chief, and urged interchangeable service between the staff and line.

Only one high-ranking officer disagreed with Upton's general views. Winfield Scott Hancock, soon to be the Democrats' presidential nominee, thought Upton's expansive army plan a mistake. He felt that the army's task was to serve as a model and a standard for the militia, a model which the states could copy in time of war. To Upton's amazement, he maintained that the duties of the soldier "are not only readily acquired by our people, but they are of such a nature that a large part of the 'national forces' are always voluntarily or under States auspices practicing them." And finally, to everyone's astonishment, Hancock advocated a reduction in the size of the army. But he stood alone; not one other witness agreed with him.

In December, 1878, after hearing all the testimony, Burnside's committee sent a bill to Congress for army reorganization. The bill called for the consolidation of the Adjutant General's Department and the Inspector General's Department into a "General Staff." The idea was originally expressed by Upton in *The Armies of Asia and Europe*, and the proposed duties of the general staff were those he had outlined. Further, the bill provided for interchangeable service in the staff and line, and for staff officers to report to the General-in-chief. Finally, it created regiments of four battalions each, with only three of the battalions being kept up to strength. The fourth would be unofficered and unmanned until needed, when national volunteers would fill the ranks and the federal government would appoint the officers. The bill was not perfect, but it came closer to meeting Upton's demands than he had dared hope.[8]

Upton was jubilant. He told Sherman, "Congress has never shown so favorable or friendly a disposition before." In urging Garfield to support it, Upton said the bill was "the wisest and best ever reported to Congress." Sherman sent Upton's remarks on to Church, who printed them in the *Journal.* Staff officers immediately denounced Upton, and he had to weather a "perfect storm of abuse." Meanwhile they were lobbying in Congress, assuring members that the bill was designed to eliminate civilian control over the military by reducing the Secretary of War to a figurehead while exalting the General-in-chief. Upton sighed, "The staff I fear will kill the bill." [9]

During the debates on the Burnside bill, Upton turned to Garfield for support. Garfield had just published two articles on army reform and his views coincided with Upton's. Upton praised the articles, "which, coming from one who has had such great experience in the field, and on the floor of Congress, cannot fail to urge public opinion toward a reform which all military men know to be of vital importance." He then told Garfield of his own current study of American military policy. Upton asked Garfield to read and criticize the completed chapters. The object of the work, he said, was "to show that instead of securing national economy by keeping the army too small, and without a proper expansive organization, we have prosecuted all of our wars with a waste of life and treasure which finds no parallel save in China." [10]

Garfield agreed to help. Since both Sherman and Du Pont were already reading the manuscript chapter by chapter, Upton now had two professional critics and one in Congress. He relied most heavily on Garfield, however, because of the latter's political connections. "I hope that you will give me the full benefit of your knowledge of the temper, and feelings of Congress, or any other body of men," he told Garfield. [11]

As Upton was working on the period following the Revolutionary War, Garfield could be of immediate help. Upton denounced the government under the Articles of Confederation because of its weakness, but praised the Constitution because it "was unqualified" in giving the central government "every war power the most despotic ruler could ask." From that point on the responsibility for any disaster which befell American arms "must lie at the doors of President and Congress." For the War of 1812, the Mexican War, and the

Civil War, the politicians were exactly the ones he intended to blame for disasters. But there was no point in irritating Congress and thus cutting off possible reform at the roots— he still had hopes for the Burnside bill. Therefore he asked Garfield to indicate the objectionable paragraphs "if I make unfortunate, or injudicious, remarks in regard to the responsibility of Congress for the many disasters that have befallen us," and he would change them.[12]

Garfield served Upton's purpose well. He praised the early chapters, which would "be of great service to Congress and the country," and urged the young officer to continue demonstrating the "wastefulness and danger" of American policy when he came to later wars. But in general Garfield served as a moderating influence on the intense Upton, suggesting that he soften his statements here and support them with more evidence there. Garfield thought that "in view of the dangers of communism" (referring to the railroad strikes of 1877) Upton's book could have a great influence.[13]

Upton soon became Garfield's staunch political supporter. In September, 1878, he congratulated the Representative on his renomination. "This Greenback craze ought to run its course within the next two years," Upton declared, "and if the Republican Party will only come out in favor of national honesty and hard money, it may yet recover all of its lost ground."[14] When Garfield was reelected, Upton celebrated with him and hoped that "we may find you the standard bearer of the party in the next great contest."[15]

But the Republicans lost seats in the off-year elections, and in early 1879 the Burnside bill went down in defeat. Upton was dismayed. Shocked by the policy followed in past wars, he despaired of ever achieving the major reforms he desired. His work went "so contrary to the current," he told Wilson, "that there is much more chance of unpopularity than popularity."[16] He feared that what he had to say would be ignored, and anyway doubted that he could say it well.

"Anyone, no matter how clever" who attempted to write on American military policy "will not only run aground, but—get stuck in the mud." [17]

Upton soon recovered from his disappointment over the failure of the Burnside bill—he did not give up his reforms easily. He had tried to break down the almost irresistible entrenchments of public indifference with a flank attack—his recommendations for American policy based on his study of foreign armies—and through legislation; now he would make another attempt, a frontal assault. He would attack the American minuteman tradition in an historical essay to show the American people that they were relying upon an ineffective force.

The only previous attempt to investigate seriously the military past of the United States had come in the 1840's when Henry Halleck wrote *The Elements of Military Art and Science*. Halleck's book was both a history of the American experience in war and a plea for reform. Upton had read the work at West Point. An early advocate of a professional army, Halleck served constantly as a guide for Upton. Halleck maintained that the lesson of military history was clear: Moderately large armies of trained men won wars quickly and at little expense, while mass armies of untrained troops either lost wars or made the winning of them excessively expensive. He emphasized the need for a trained soldiery and quoted Washington at length to discredit the militia. Facing the problem of popular aversion to a large standing army, Halleck recommended an expansive army centered around the regulars. He also proposed internal army reforms which corresponded with those Upton asked for.

Halleck wrote before the Mexican War, and he never analyzed either it or the Civil War in any systematic fashion. But he made it clear that the Civil War strengthend his feelings about professional as opposed to civilian officers. In April, 1863, he told a friend, "The great difficulty we have to contend with is *poor, poorer, worthless* officers. Many of them have neither judgment, sense nor courage. And I almost despair of any improvement. Recent appointments are worse if anything than before. Politics! Politics! They are utterly ruining the country." A year later, after damning Nathaniel P. Banks and Benjamin F. Butler, two civilian generals, Halleck asked rhetorically, "If the President were to appoint soldiers, or merchants, or farmers as judges on the Supreme Bench, how would the law be administered, and the interests of the United States protected?" [18]

Upton accepted Halleck's ideas. Before he even began his research he had his thesis. He agreed with Halleck that the military policy of the United States was a "crime," and promised Wilson he would trace it from the Revolution through the Civil War "to show at what expense and treasure and blood a nation must prosecute wars" as long as it neglected to erect a solid military organization. To Du Pont he explained that his purpose was to "expose the folly and criminality" of American policy, which was "essentially Chinese in its character." [19]

Upton hoped to bring enough influence to bear to effect a fundamental change in the system, but despaired of success because he saw himself caught in a dilemma. If he "severely quoted history" as he should, he would so damn the militia that it would cause "an uproar [that would] destroy the value of the book." But if he did not, Congress would see no reason to change the system. Still he plodded along, gathering the facts. [20]

As Upton became more pessimistic his friends tried to encourage him. Sherman urged him on while praising the chapters he had read. [21] Upton doubted that his friends were serious. He told Du Pont that he feared Sherman and Garfield were "unwilling to express openly their dessent." [22]

Upton convinced himself that no one really agreed with his ideas, and he began to see himself as a misunderstood prophet standing alone against a hostile world. "I do not hope for any immediate results," he told Du Pont, "except unlimited abuse." [23] He feared that his strictures against the militia and States' Rights would "raise a storm which no single individual could withstand." [24]

By June of 1880 Upton had finished the campaigns of 1862. He expected to cover the remainder of the Civil War with little difficulty and hoped to finish soon. But shortly thereafter he decided to drop his work on American military policy and engage in other activity for a time. His excuse was that he would wait for the outcome of the 1880 Presidential campaign. If Garfield won, Upton would try to publish the book in 1881, but if the Democrats gained control of the White House he would wait four years for publication because "there will be too much anti-state sovereignty in it [the book] to please them." [25]

Actually, Upton dropped the work just short of completion because of the one fear of his life—fear of failure. If he published the book and no legislation resulted, as had happened with *The Armies of Asia and Europe* (which had sold less than 600 copies), he would no longer be able to see himself as a reformer. Better to pose as a much-maligned prophet who would be roundly denounced if he made his views known.

Despite Garfield's victory in the Presidential contest, Upton did not return to his work. In late 1880 he was transferred to California, and meanwhile he started another revision of his tactics. Shortly after he arrived in California he died; "Military Policy" remained uncompleted. Henry du Pont had possession of it, and he saw to its circulation among prominent army officers. Thus even before its eventual publication in the twentieth century, "The Military Policy of the

United States" influenced the thinking of professional soldiers in America, even if it did not lead to reforms until after the Spanish-American War.

In his introduction Upton said that his purpose was "to treat historically and statistically, our military policy . . . and to show the enormous and unnecessary sacrifice of life and treasure, which has attended all our armed struggles." All American wars had been prolonged because of a lack of preparation, caused by an "unfounded jealousy" of even a small standing army, the persistent use of raw militia, the absence of an expansive organization, the bounty and substitute systems, excessive state influence, and "a variety of other defects." In the introduction he dwelt on two themes: the prejudice against standing armies, which was both unreasonable and dangerous, and the great and unnecessary length of American wars.

In his most famous statement Upton declared that "twenty thousand regular troops at Bull Run would have routed the insurgents, settled the question of military resistance, and relieved us from the pain and suspense of four years of war." In part, Upton was playing a numbers game (in the text he said 10,000 regulars would have sufficed),[26] but actually he here demonstrated his own major failing. All of Upton's recommendations and dictums—indeed, almost all of his adult life—aimed at a single end, the creation of a modern, professional army in the United States. But because he failed to appreciate the interrelationship between politics and the armed forces in a democracy, Upton was incapable of seeing that he could not merely graft a professional army onto the American system.[27] For example, he was aware of the threat to the regular army implicit in the States' Rights position, and consequently was a strong nationalist, but rather than try to win southerners and Democrats over to his position, or make some adjustments to suit them, he was content to hope for a Republican victory and a resulting triumph of nationalism. Unfortunately for him, States' Righters could always count on a sizable block of Senate seats. Upton, for all his concern with the effects of his writing on Congressional sensibilities, never even tried to work out a system which could both give America a professional army and satisfy the States' Righters.

His error was well illustrated in his dictum about the regulars at Bull Run.* The thesis assumed that it could have been possible to alter one factor in a complex situation while leaving all others unchanged. Twenty thousand regulars probably could have won the war on that hot July day in 1861, but to have placed that many on the field would have required an army of at least 50,000 men. A regular army of that size could have had only one purpose—to coerce the South†—and the fear of one section using the army to coerce another was the precise reason the Founding Fathers had put their faith in a state-controlled militia.[28]

Further, as had been true of *The Armies of Asia and Europe*, Upton failed to show the American people why they needed a modern armed force. The militia had remained "the

---

* Europeans agreed with Upton. The Prince de Joinville, an unofficial French observer at McClellan's headquarters, said of the Americans, "In Europe . . . we have learned to recognize the comparative value of the regular soldier, and of this costly and capricious amateur soldier, who is called a volunteer. An army of sixty thousand regulars would have done more than double or triple the number of volunteers; but in America they do not know this, and besides, they do not wish to know it. It would involve a renunciation of the general and deeply rooted creed, that every American, when he wishes to do a thing, may find within himself, without any apprenticeship, the power to do it." Quoted in Jay Luvaas, *The Military Legacy of the Civil War: The European Inheritance* (Chicago, 1959), 82.

† Upton said at one point that the North should have attacked in the fall of 1861, but did not because "to save a million or two of dollars" it had never hired spies, and so knew nothing of the real situation in the South. The immediate question: on whom would the spies have spied before 1861? Emory Upton, *The Military Policy of the United States* (Washington, 1904), 313.

first line of defense" because, although most observers realized that it needed drastic reforming, there was no need for it to defend against anything. Nineteenth-century Americans relied upon an ineffective force which protected them from a nonexistent threat. Upton saw that the threat lay in the future, but he could not or would not convince the public.

Upton concluded his introduction with specific recommendations for a new system. The military forces of the United States should consist of the regular army, the National Volunteers which would be trained and officered by the regulars on the expansive system, and the militia, to enforce the laws and suppress insurrections. His system contained nothing new. Most of his recommendations had been advocated at one time or another by various army officers, and the expansive principle dated to at least 1821 and John C. Calhoun's report as Secretary of War. Upton's insistence on a nationally controlled army had been anticipated by many, most recently Halleck. What Upton did was to systematize in a coherent form ideas which most professional soldiers shared.[29]

In the text Upton presented most of his recommendations in a negative fashion. After discussing each war, he listed the lessons the student should take from it. Each lesson pointed up a fault in the system which should be corrected. The Revolutionary War demonstrated that statesmen who were inexperienced in military affairs should not attempt to direct the army; that a confederation was the weakest of all forms of government; that proportionally as the general government gave the states authority to arm and organize troops it lessened the military strength of the whole people; that disciplined troops were at least twice as good as raw ones; that a nation could not rely upon voluntary enlistments; that regular troops were the only safe reliance of the government and the only agency which could preserve freedom; and that trained officers were indispensable for an effective army.

The heroes of the Revolutionary War were the regular officers who held the army together by their "devotion to discipline." During the war the regulars went without pay, food, shelter, and clothes without complaining, while the militia mutinied and deserted. The conclusion was inescapable; the real enemy of freedom in America was the militia, not a standing army. The villains in the war were the militia and the pernicious doctrine of States' Rights.

Upton presented his case through the words of George Washington, making only occasional comments himself. He quoted Washington's strictures against the militia often and in full confidence—the Father of his country could not be assailed. "They come in," Washington said of the militia, "you cannot tell how; go, you cannot tell when; and act, you cannot tell where; consume your provisions, exhaust your stores and leave you at last at a critical moment." Sherman approved of Upton's approach. He told Garfield, "I like Upton's method of connecting Washington's testimony so as to make a logical and connected chain." [30]

Because of the extreme vulnerability of Upton's reliance upon Washington and because of the later discovery of new documents, Upton's severest critics have maintained that his chapter on the Revolution was the key to his work and have concentrated their attacks in this area.[31] Upton had used the Jared Sparks edition of Washington's writings and had neglected to consult any manuscripts; in the twentieth century John M. Palmer discovered in the National Archives Washington's "Sentiments on a Peace Establishment." In it Washington indicated that he favored a well-organized militia, not a standing army of any size. Upton had failed to recognize that the Militia Act of 1792 suggested—although it did not require—an organized militia in each state, in accordance with Washington's wishes.

Since the discovery of "Sentiments on a Peace Establishment," Palmer and his fellow critics have raged against Upton's misinterpretation of Washington. Upton, Palmer said, made Washington "his principal witness in behalf of a scheme [the expansible army] that Washington never heard of and one which was diametrically opposed to everything that he ever proposed." [32] Another critic, Frederick P. Todd, accused Upton of failing to distinguish between state volunteers, such as fought in the Mexican and Civil Wars, and common militia. The charge simply was not true. Upton saw and applauded the difference—volunteers could serve outside the state and enlisted for a period of years rather than months—but he still opposed any state control. Todd, an authority on the National Guard, bemoaned the fact that "no other book [referring to *The Military Policy of the United States*] has had such a profound effect upon American military policy," and demonstrated that regular army officers worshipped Upton and used his arguments to stop the flow of money to the Guard.[33]

Upton's attitudes toward militia and state volunteers were more complex than his critics acknowledged. Commenting on the Militia Act of 1792, Upton praised it for its enunciation of the "truly democratic doctrine that every able-bodied male citizen owed military service to his country," but found that in general the bill was inadequate because it left too much power in the hands of the states. Many legislatures ignored their duties, while others, "totally ignorant of the first principles of the military art," misspent their money. The result was that instead of one efficient army, America had thirteen bad ones. "View it in whatever light we may," he concluded, "the conversion of the militia into an army of the first line, as designed by the law, was a wild and impracticable scheme." [34] The reason was state control. Upton had no objection to militia as such—his National Volunteers were militia operating under federal authority and directed by the army—but he did object to state militia.

Seemingly, the War of 1812 proved Upton's contention about the state militia. The raw troops proved worthless and caused a long series of humiliating defeats. The Battle of New Orleans, far from salvaging the militia's reputation, only showed that with trained officers in command, effective artillery in support, and works so formidable that it would have required a regular siege to carry them, even militia could halt an assault launched by a blundering, incompetent opponent.

Not even Sherman could accept so partisan a view. In a comment on the chapter, he pointed out that other short-comings hurt the American cause, including "want of skill by generals and officers, want of concert of action and dispersion of our strength, . . . want of men of action as leaders." [35]

The Mexican War brought a "revolution" in American military policy by substituting volunteers for militia, and despite his critics Upton realized the difference between the two. He had many kind words to say about the volunteers and their conduct on the battlefield, especially at Buena Vista (where, he hastened to point out, those who did the fighting had been undergoing field training for eight months), but he also had many criticisms. The worst feature of the bill which authorized the President to accept volunteers was the section which allowed them to choose to serve for either one year or the duration. This led to the acceptance of too many volunteers (the vast majority served for only one year), wasted effort in transportation and training, and caused unnecessary expense. The twelve-month enlistment policy was also dangerous. Scott had to remain on the defensive at Cerro Gordo for two months after sending seven of eleven regiments of volunteer infantry home when their terms expired. If the Mexicans could have attacked while Scott waited for reinforcements, they would have destroyed the regular army of the United States. Long-term enlistments for one-quarter the number of volunteers would have been a better system.

Upton objected to the "costly mistake" of regarding the volunteers as militia and allowing the governors of the states to appoint their officers.[36] One of the two major themes of his treatment of the Civil War was the evil effect of state influence on the army. Governors had the power to send short-term volunteers into the field without a single officer of military education and experience to lead them. "In no monarchy or despotism of the Old World," Upton commented, "do the laws give to the ruler such power to do evil." The military legislation of 1861, based on the erroneous theory that the United States was a confederation and not a nation, gave control to the states and the power of promotion to the governors, which discouraged good service in the field and encouraged corruption at home. To seek promotion, officers left their posts in the field to exert their influence at the state capitals, while those who remained faithful to their duty "had the mortification of seeing many worthless officers . . . come back to the field with increased rank and command." The situation of the regular army officer without political influence who served with the volunteer forces beggared description.[37]

A much better system, Upton maintained, would have been to reduce the regular army to a cadre and disperse its officers among the volunteers. Then every regiment of volunteer infantry, cavalry, and artillery could have had a trained officer for its leader, and a large and efficient army would have been created in three months. By refusing to adopt this policy (which both the General-in-chief and the Adjutant General, fearing to ruin the regular army, opposed), the nation wasted the talents of its regular officers and the courage of its volunteers.[38]

The Confederacy followed a more sensible policy. While the North attempted to "save the Union by fighting as a

Confederacy, the Confederates sought to destroy it by fighting as a nation." The South abandoned States' Rights, took away from the governors the power to appoint and promote officers and to organize new regiments, and adopted conscription. These policies saved the Confederacy in the spring of 1862 when their twelve-months volunteers were about to melt away. "If our legislators will but study the lesson, it may yet in the remote future teach them how to rescue and defend our liberty and independence." [39]

Upton's second major theme in his treatment of the Civil War was the danger of allowing civilians, especially the Secretary of War, to exercise too much power—almost, he inferred, of allowing him any power at all. Edwin Stanton, Secretary of War under Lincoln and Andrew Johnson, was the first powerful wartime Secretary in American history. His actions disturbed the great majority of regular army officers. After the war the professionals made various attempts to curb the power of the Secretary. In January, 1866, General-in-chief Grant suggested to Stanton that all orders from the Secretary to the army go through the General-in-chief's office, and the day after he became President Grant ordered his Secretary of War, John M. Schofield, to direct the chiefs of the staff corps, departments, and bureaus to report to and act under the orders of the General-in-chief. The various staffs, however, having built up their virtual independence through the years, resisted the order and Congress revoked it in 1869. Over the next decade the Secretary, usually William W. Belknap, and the General-in-chief, Sherman, fought with one another over lines of authority, with the Secretary usually winning. The bureau chiefs and the staff remained responsibile to the Secretary, who thus retained enormous power.[40]

In his attacks on the Secretary of War, Upton was not breaking new ground. But here, as in so many other areas, he was providing historical justification for the assault. The

Revolutionary War and the War of 1812, Upton said, showed that the position was inherently dangerous, "especially whenever a citizen of military experience has been at the head of the War Department," because he was tempted to exercise military command. The inherent dangers in the position of the Secretary became real ones in 1862, the year in which the North should have won the war but, because of the meddlings of Stanton, so blundered that it made a long conflict necessary.[41] "If you want to know who was the cause of a three years' war after we created a disciplined army of 600,000 men," Upton told Du Pont, "it was Stanton." But, he emphasized, Stanton did not create the system —it created Stanton.[42]

Trouble began on March 11, 1862, when Lincoln dispensed with General-in-chief George B. McClellan and ordered all commanders to report to the Secretary of War. Thus command of the vast armies which were just then ready to strike passed from the "hands of an educated soldier" to Lincoln and Stanton, "neither of whom professed any knowledge of the military art." Lincoln's order was based on the "defect of our laws"—the constitutional provision that made the President the commander in chief—which "tempted the President to assume the character and responsibilities of a military commander" and allowed him to pass that authority on to the Secretary of War. Stanton, rather than organizing, recruiting, and supplying the armies, tried to revise the plans of military commanders, disastrously splitting McClellan's forces before the Peninsular campaign and making success impossible.[43]

Upton maintained that the Secretary had no right to exercise any military command because his duties were administrative. He realized that his attacks on the Secretary would not be popular, because the public regarded him as the guardian of civilian control over the army. But Upton pointed out, referring to the Andrew Johnson-Stanton imbroglio, "when our President has been impeached by the House for attempting to remove a Secretary who claimed that his orders were the President's orders, I think it time that some one should present his position to the army in its proper light." [44]

To give added weight to his contention, Upton presented McClellan as a military genius. This ran counter to the general feeling in the army; as Upton told Du Pont, "It may astonish you that I now regard McClellan, in his military character, as a much-abused man," but it fit well with Upton's thesis. Lincoln removed McClellan because of his politics, but the differences between the general and the President would never have arisen "but for the interference of Stanton." The Secretary of War was "at the bottom" of all subsequent disasters because of his tendency to "usurp military command." [45]

Upton did not easily embrace McClellan. A prewar abolitionist, Upton had sympathized with the Radical Republicans. When the Democrat McClellan, after being relieved from command, rode down the lines of the army, Upton was one of the few who did not join in the cheers. But, he told Garfield, his research had convinced him that McClellan had done excellent work in the war and failed to reap the success he deserved because of the interferences of Stanton.[46] Upton did admit that McClellan had mistakenly tried to influence the political results of the war, but hastened to add that although soldiers should not interfere in politics, "they alone can be held responsible for the control and direction of our armies in the field." [47]

Though he could not openly advocate such a system, what Upton was contending for through his attacks on the Secretary of War was a complete independence of the General-in-chief—and thereby the army—from civilian control. Impressed with the Prussian war machine, Upton hoped that the American army could achieve a similar position. He concealed his aspiration well by paying due deference to the office of the President and he was willing enough to allow the President to be titular commander in chief. But his remarks about the "defect" in the Constitution which "tempted" the President to "assume the character . . . of a military commander" clearly indicated Upton's feelings." [48]

In sum, Upton denounced the military policy of the United States as one of weakness and folly. Framed by Congress and executed by the President and Secretary of War, it was dominated by uninformed civilians. Although it did allow a superb regular army, it kept that army's duties, responsibilities, and powers pitifully small. In wartime, it attempted to supplement the army with a citizen soldiery whom history had shown to be thoroughly undependable. The militia system and state control aggravated the defects, and when the militia's futility became obvious, it resorted to a volunteer system which retained most of the faults of the militia. In the Mexican and Civil Wars the American military policy brought forth a good army only at an excessive cost in time, money, and lives. America needed a self-controlled, professional, expansive army.

Upton was looking to the past in order to avoid having to come to terms with the future. He was not merely ignoring the one clear lesson of the Civil War; he was trying to stand the lesson on its head. The Civil War proved that in future wars civilians, be they the head of a federation, a nation, a union, or a confederacy, would lead the masses into combat while the professional soldiers would serve only as *one* of the tools used by the civilians. Stanton and Lincoln (and Jefferson Davis) were not "usurpers"; they were part of an historic development—a development Upton refused to acknowledge.

He was not alone. European observers of the Civil War concentrated their criticism on the American lack of preparation, regular forces, a general staff, and the nonprofessionalism of the armies. For the Prussians, the American conflict was not worthy of serious study because, lacking discipline, good officers, and a general staff, the Civil War armies were by their very nature responsible for the lack of decisive victories "and the 'unnatural' duration of the war." [49] The Franco-Prussian War, coming shortly after the Civil War, made it possible for the professionals to believe that short wars, fought by highly trained forces led by educated soldiers, were once again in the ascendancy. To so believe, they had to concentrate on the early Prussian victories in 1870 and ignore the surprising resistance of the people's war Leon Gambetta unleashed after Sedan. They did.

The master knew better. General Moltke, head of the Prussian General Staff, sadly declared, "It is all wrong to lead whole peoples against each other. That is not progress, but a return to barbarism," but he saw that it was inevitable.[50]

The nature of modern war was described most clearly by the Jacobin orator Bertrand Barère de Vieuzac who, when arguing for the *levee en masse* of 1793, cried, "Let everyone assume his post in the national and military effort that is preparing. The young men shall fight; the married men shall forge weapons and transport supplies; the women will make tents and serve in the hospitals; the children will make up old linen into lint; the old men will have themselves carried into the public squares to rouse the courage of the fighting men, and to preach hatred of kings and the unity of the Republic. The public buildings shall be turned into barracks, the public squares into munitions factories; the earthen floors of cellars shall be treated with lye to extract saltpetre."

In part, Upton saw and appreciated this development— thus his demand for universal conscription as a democratic device for raising armies—but his regular army, backed by the National Volunteers, did not meet the new situation. In Barère's words, the soldiers had become citizens and the citizens (all of them) soldiers, which created a whole new set of problems for the professional soldier—problems with which Upton's proposed system never came to grips.[51]

Upton's system was deficient because, although he saw the democratic revolution in war and realized what most of its effects would be, he did not like it. Rather he preferred the old methods, when violence had been monopolized by regular armies while civilians—including Presidents and Secretaries of War—had watched, respectfully and from a distance.

Therefore Upton, like most of the military of the Western world, hailed the Franco-Prussian War as the overture to the future. By ignoring the American Civil War (or explaining that it would have ended in 1862 if the civilians had not interfered), professional soldiers interpreted the Prussian victory of 1870 to mean that the democratic and civilian revolution in warfare had been brought under control and that regular armies—with trained civilian reserves *under* them—would again dominate the battlefield. Thus the Franco-Prussian War became "natural," the Civil War "unnatural."

Upton's thinking was far ahead of that of his fellow professionals. They expected the next war would, following the pattern of 1870, be a short one, with no interference from the "frocks." The Germans, well on their way to creating a mass army, never realized that eventually civilians would wrest control of the civilian army from them. German soldiers thought that by eliminating the Landwehr and placing control of the army in their own hands, they could avoid civilian interference and still have a mass army. They were wrong. Civilian control came late to Germany, but when it came it was with a vengeance—Hitler completely dominated the army. The French, who had a warning in 1871 with Gambetta, did see what might happen to a mass army, and almost unconsciously feared it. Upton, who had fought in and studied the war which provided the clearest example, fully realized the dangers to his profession inherent in the mass army.

Still, he wanted the mass army; his dream was to create it while avoiding civilian control. The whole point of his study of the military policy of the United States was not, then, to attack the militia—that was a feint. He wanted a militia, that is, some form of civilian reserve, but he wanted it under professional control. His attack was on civilian domination, be it state or federal; his hope was that after the elimination of state control the federal government, because of his assault on Stanton, would not impose its control. Upton's reform program was progressive in almost every detail, and reactionary in sum.

Death

"As I have full faith in all the promises of our Lord and Savior Jesus Christ, and am firmly convinced that to die is gain, I desire that no person may wear mourning for me for a period exceeding one year." Emory Upton, Last Will and Testament.

Through the first forty years of his life Emory Upton had been an optimist. He approached both his personal problems and those of the army in the spirit of a recent graduate, fully expecting to do the difficult immediately and the impossible shortly. His battle at Columbus symbolized his approach to life; the mad dash up to the problem, the rapid scanning of it, the quick decision, and then the successful action. His insatiable appetite for work combined with his reform impulse to carry him through the war, the *Tactics*, the report on the armies of Asia and Europe, and most of the military policy study.

But by 1879 Upton was becoming a bitter, disillusioned, tired man suffering from increasingly severe neuroses. He still tried to approach problems as he always had, but now his assaults were falling short. The failure of the Burnside bill had been a major defeat. A worse insult was that, although he was convinced that what he had to say was vital to the security of the country, the public ignored him. Upton began to imagine that a conspiracy had been formed against him and to feel that his enemies would rather see the United States humiliated in the next war than to adopt his reforms. As his frustration grew, he withdrew into himself. He turned his bitterness and anger inward and, for the first time in his life, Emory Upton began to doubt himself. The result was tragedy.

Upton began to see himself as a failure, but he really did not have even that masochistic pleasure. He was not denounced or vilified, he was just ignored. The public, if it thought of him at all, remembered Upton as a gallant Civil War officer who for some unaccountable reason had stayed in the army after 1865. All of his talk about the "storm of abuse" that would descend upon him if he published the military policy study was wishful thinking—abuse would be better than indifference.

At Fortress Monroe, Upton became more inclined to mull over his past triumphs and less eager to face the future. A comrade in arms from the 1865 campaign who visited him noted that Upton had gained weight and was "older looking." The two soldiers reminisced over the Wilson raid. Upton said he "would like to commute the rest of his life for six months of just such military service." [1]

At the same time, Upton began to avoid others. His sister Sara kept house for him, and she insisted upon a punctilious discharge of his social obligations, but aside from his semi-official duties he entertained little. Only Wilson and Du Pont were really welcome. Sara usually spent the summer months in New York State, and in July and August Upton lived alone, receiving no guests. He did retain his sense of responsibility. He exacted the strictest discipline from his troops, forced his officers and their wives to give religious instruction to the men, and required everyone to attend Sunday services. To set the best example of soldierly conduct, he carried himself with dignity and aloofness.[2]

Upton's closet friend was Henry du Pont. The two old classmates visited each other whenever possible, and Upton always looked forward to his stays at Winterthur, the Du Pont family estate near Wilmington, Delaware. In 1877 Du Pont's first child, Catherine, died, and the two men drew even closer to each other through their experience of each having suffered a severe loss. Upton assured Du Pont that he would find consolation in the message of Easter and said they could both look forward to meeting their loved ones again. Continuing in a reflective mood, Upton attempted to analyze his relationship to Du Pont. "I think as we grow older we manifest less disposition to make new friends," he decided, "and as a consequence cling with the greater tenacity to those made in early life."[3]

The year that Catherine died, Du Pont's wife had another daughter, Louise. Next to his nephew and namesake, Emory Upton Alexander, Louise was Upton's favorite. He played with her often when he was at Winterthur and frequently gave her presents. "My friendship for children I fear will rapidly increase to idolatry," he confessed to Du Pont. Occasionally he persuaded his sister to leave her son, Emory Alexander, with him at Fortress Monroe for a week or so. He always pestered her to leave the boy longer and more often.[4]

His only other interests were in the army and its affairs, such as the Fitz-John Porter case. In 1863 General Porter, one of McClellan's favorite officers, had been tried and found guilty of a "willful failure to obey orders" during the Second Bull Run campaign. Radical Republicans, in an attempt to discredit McClellan, charged that the Democrat Porter had deliberately neglected to support the Republican General John Pope in the battle and thereby caused his defeat. Porter was cashiered. Upton interpreted the incident as another example of the politicians' illogical hatred of the regular army—Porter was a West Point graduate—and supported Porter in his attempts to exonerate himself. In 1878 an army board examined the case and recommended remission of the sentence. Upton urged his Congressional ally, Garfield, to accept the board's findings and to influence Congress to do the same. But Garfield refused and Congress took no action. Upton was certain that Garfield's motives were political, that he was unwilling to reverse what had been essentially a party decision. "Always a Republican, I desire simply to see justice done," Upton explained to Garfield. "The great party has saved the Union, and can well afford to restore to honor a man who has fought so gallantly for his country." Still, Congress did nothing for Porter during Upton's lifetime.[5]

Minutiae occupied much of Upton's time. Army and militia officers "who study the showy side of the military profession" bombarded him with questions about his drill system. He sent one example along to Du Pont. An artillery officer asked some dozen questions, such as, "at command, 'Raise' in loading with or without the numbers, does No. 1 have his left arm horizontal over the piece in the direction of the left trunnion . . . until he continues to execute the second motion—or does he move his arm over in the direction of the left trunnion and bring it to a rest by his left side before he commences the execution of the 2nd motion?" Despite the burden it imposed, Upton tried to answer hundreds of such inquiries.[6]

Meanwhile, Upton convinced himself that, with or without a Republican victory, the publication of his military policy manuscript would do no good. He therefore turned his attention back to tactics—the one field in which his efforts as a reformer had been successful. Up to 1880 he had drawn on his tour only for inspiration for organizational reform; now he hoped to use his observations to improve his tactical system. He had seen the company column used in maneuvers in India, Italy, Russia, and Austria, and thought he could "produce a system better than any which has thus far been presented." He proposed to use the basic idea of the company column, but to modify it by adding deployment by numbers. He would reduce the size of the column by using a double column in each company. He also wanted to attack another problem. He told Sherman, "You are aware that thus far in our history tactics, in all areas of the service, have been simply a collection of rules for passing from one formation to another. How to fight has been left to actual experience in war." In his revision, Upton would correct that deficiency.[7]

In 1874 Upton had criticized the Prussian company because it was too large—255 men to a company as opposed to the American 100—and therefore unwieldy. After seeing the larger companies in action and conceiving of the possibility of half-company columns, however, Upton reversed himself. He called for a peacetime company of 66 men with three officers, and a wartime company of 216 men with five officers. The companies would move into battle in double column, so that each column would be only slightly larger than the old American company of 100 men. His method of fighting remained basically the same, although he emphasized even more strongly than before the need for a heavy skirmish line. A four-company battalion would go into battle with two companies feeding men into the skirmish line in units of four, while two companies remained in reserve. He also called for a three-battalion regiment. At that time, and until after the Spanish-American War, the American army had a cumbersome one-battalion regiment. Upton wanted three battalions to a regiment because the increased range of both infantry and artillery necessitated an open order, which was difficult if not impossible to attain with a one-battalion regiment. Under Upton's new system, junior officers would have to handle more men than before. Therefore he again emphasized, as he had so often in the past, the need for more advanced and rigorous officer training. He also wanted every enlisted man in the army to be well versed in skirmish drill, and urged constant practice in it.

Upton approached Sherman with his ideas on revision, and Sherman arranged for a meeting. When Upton walked into the General-in-chief's office, he found Sherman's brother-in-law, General Charles Ewing, and General John Schofield in the room. Ewing said to Upton, "I never witnessed your skirmish-drill till a day or two ago, and I want to tell you it is the prettiest thing I ever saw."

Schofield added, "Did you read the account of a recent lecture delivered in London before the United Service Institution? The lecturer presented what he called the best formation for skirmishing, when Sir Garnet Wolseley stated that the proposed method was the same as the American system."

Sherman turned to Upton and remarked, "Yes, that was your invention." Upton thanked him, then outlined his new proposals. Sherman responded, "You revise it, bring it to me, and I will get it approved."

Upton soon had his ideas on paper and began sending them around to fellow officers for criticism. Meanwhile he urged Congressmen to present a bill for the three-battalion regiment and the four-company battalion. He told Church, whose *Journal* was read by most members of the Congressional military affairs committees, that if he could get the organization he wanted he could "adapt the deployment by numbers in such a manner as to give us the simplest and best skirmish drill extant." The old ambition still flared up occasionally. Upton felt that he had framed a system which was so good that it would soon be adopted throughout the world. But, as usual, he despaired of getting the necessary legislation from the American Congress, and he did not.[8]

In April of 1879 Lieutenant Colonel Upton went to Washington to discuss his chances of promotion with War Department officials. He found that they had "given everything" to the infantry and cavalry on the plea that those arms needed young colonels. Upton was not satisfied with the excuse; his own regiment, now the Fourth U. S. Artillery, had furnished troops for the last three Indian wars; each time they fought under a captain. He complained that an "injustice" had been done to him.[9]

By February, 1880, Upton had decided that "there is no prospect of my promotion till we get a law of compulsory retirement," because the General-in-chief would put no one on the retired list against his will. In the American army, line officers received their promotions on a regimental basis. A second lieutenant could move up to first lieutenant or a lieutenant colonel to colonel only when a vacancy occurred in his regiment. Promotion was uneven; some officers moved up fast, others not at all. Many lieutenants had to wait twenty-five to thirty years for their captains to die before they could be promoted. There was no compulsory retirement law and most senior officers stayed on the active list tion based on zeal and merit, not on length of service in the army as a lieutenant, set in the post-Civil War period, is thirty-two years. One of Upton's recommendations in *The Armies of Asia and Europe* had been for faster promotion based on zeal and merit, not on length of service in a particular regiment. In part, the promotion problem also involved his call for interchangeable service in the staff and line, because staff officers received one promotion immediately upon joining their department, and thereafter moved ahead faster than the line officers.[10]

By March, 1880, Upton was filled with frustration. He could not finish his military policy study, get Congress to pass any bill looking toward either general army reform or tactical innovation, or receive a promotion. Always a man

of nervous temperament, he began to develop acute physical disorders. A mild sinus condition, or nasal catarrh, had
become troublesome, and he was attacked by violent headaches. Upton went to see Dr. Harrison Allen in Philadelphia.
He told the doctor, "Cure me of this, and I will give you ten
thousand dollars!"

Dr. Allen treated Upton with electrical cauterization of the
mucous membrane of the nasal passages. He placed a fine
coiled wire upon the membrane and caused it to glow at a
high temperature by sending a spark through it. Allen
hoped that this would restore the suppressed circulation of
the membrane. He could find no connection between Upton's
sinus condition and his headaches.

Dr. Allen told Upton that with six weeks of daily treatment he could cure the sinus condition; Upton took a three
months leave to go to Philadelphia for the treatment. The
electrical cauterization was painful, and although it did help
the sinus condition it did nothing to ease the headaches.
Upton's mind was becoming clouded and his thoughts confused. He realized that he was irritable and snappish, so he
told no one of his presence in Philadelphia, preferring to live
entirely alone. Allen examined Upton repeatedly, hoping
to find some cause of the headaches, but he was unsuccessful. He later conjectured that Upton might have had a tumor
growing in the remote recesses of the face which was attacking the brain.[11]

Despite his pain and confusion, Upton continued to drive
himself. His current professional interest was with the question of compulsory retirement, and he began to put pressure
on editor Church to support such a proposal. Upton said that
he could not openly advocate compulsory retirement, because the colonel of the Fourth Artillery was over 62 and
Upton stood to gain from the bill. He asked Church to write
editorials in the *Journal* favoring the policy. Upton said that
"in the staff where sitting round is the chief occupation

age doesn't make so much difference," but it did in the line.
When Church hesitated, Upton pressed harder. He asked
when Church would take up the subject, and added, "Every
body in the army wants it, except those who are over . . .
the age of sixty-two." Church printed a strong article on
compulsory retirement, and Upton thanked him.[12]

With Church on his side, Upton felt he could come out
in the open. In March he published "Facts in Favor of
Compulsory Retirement" in *The United Service Magazine.*
In it Upton repeated many of the arguments Henry Halleck
had used in the 1840's. Upton began by listing the successful
generals of the past. From Philip of Macedon to Napoleon
he found that they were all young, aggressive men, usually
under forty years of age. In the American army, however,
"greybeards" commanded. They usually absented themselves
during wars, allowing younger men to take on their duties
and responsibilities, then returned to the army in peacetime.
This forced the younger officers to revert back to their permanent, lower rank. "The age of man between twenty and
forty is the age of aggression," Upton contended. "It is during this period that he likes to encounter obstacles for the
pleasure of vanquishing them." In the American army, however, few if any line officers became majors, much less
colonels or generals, before they were forty.

Upton proposed a compulsory retirement bill which would
force officers onto the retired list when they reached sixty-
two years of age. He pointed out that the retirement of one
colonel would lead to promotion for a lieutenant colonel,
a major, a captain, a 1st lieutenant, and a 2nd lieutenant. A
compulsory retirement bill would therefore be highly encouraging to every young officer in the country. It would not
do as much good as a bill which would base promotion on
zeal and merit, but it would be some help. Upton concluded
by saying that the lieutenants and captains of the army were
not "greedy for promotion," but in view of their capacity,

"they do ask that they shall have a chance to be colonels at least eight years before reaching the age of threescore-and-ten." [13]

Church praised Upton for the article. Upton thanked him, then said, "lineal promotion is the next step." But retirement had to be settled first. "I hear I am roundly abused by those who hope to die in service," Upton added.[14]

He was. One officer, writing to *The Army and Navy Journal*, complained that Upton stole his entire article from Halleck, who had written when he was a young man. The critic then pointed out that later Halleck himself, when he was General-in-chief during the Civil War, replaced McClellan with an older man, Burnside, and again with an older one, Hooker, and then again when Meade succeeded Hooker. This disproved both Halleck's and Upton's theories that young men always rose in long wars due to their superior vigor and energy.[15] Another correspondent added, "It so turns out that the greatest soldier of Europe, General Moltke, is a living refutation of the compulsory retirement doctrine." [16]

Meanwhile Upton had other worries. He had finished his duties at the Artillery School and in June, 1880, the War Department ordered him to join his regiment. Upton had not served in the field since he left for West Point as Commandant in 1870. The Fourth U. S. Artillery was stationed at the Presidio, near San Francisco, California. Upton wanted to stay in Philadelphia until Dr. Allen could finish his treatments, and asked for a two-month extension of his leave.[17] The War Department granted his request. Then, in July, the colonel of the Fourth Artillery died and the Department gave Upton command of the regiment.

Late in 1880 Upton, although his treatments were not finished, decided he could delay no longer and traveled overland to California. By early 1881 he was settled at the Presidio. His quarters faced San Francisco Bay, two miles away, and he enjoyed listening to the roar of the surf at night. But he soon found himself in an altercation with the Departmental commander, Major General Irvin McDowell. McDowell had his headquarters in San Francisco, and Upton complained that "there is not an expenditure of five dollars at any post in the harbor that he does not personally superintend." Upton claimed that McDowell directed the construction of every house on the post, down to selecting the color they were painted.

Although his sinus condition and headaches were still painful, whenever he could Upton ignored them to attend to his duties. When the men of his regiment put on a play, he made an appearance. But when a fellow officer asked his opinion of the performance, he replied that he could form none. His head pained him so much that he had no remembrance at all of the first act.

Upton also managed to go to San Francisco on the public occasions which required his presence. Once, at a dinner, he bragged to his civilian companion that his new tactical system would eliminate war. When the civilian looked dubious, Upton explained that his system was so perfect that, given two countries and their resources, the result of a conflict between them could be calculated with mathematical certainty. Thus there would be no more war.

Upton usually stayed on the post and led a solitary life. He found the walks around the Presidio appealing and took frequent advantage of them. It helped ease his headaches, which had mounted to a steady, intense throbbing.[18] The pain was often so great that he could not sleep at night and it was practically impossible for him to concentrate on any mental task. He had periods in which he could not think rationally and responsibly. He began to consider death as a welcome release.

Ever since he had lost Emily, Upton had been fascinated with death. In 1872 he confessed to his father, "I love to meditate on the heavenly city where Christ dwells, and is the light of those who believe in His mercy. . . . If our lives are spent in glorifying God . . . [they] will in death be quickened, and again blossom in eternal loveliness, and ripen in the continual sunshine of God's love. Purified, we shall then be as the images of the heavenly." A year and a half later he dealt with the same theme. "I love to dwell upon the glories of the unseen world, where, all being in harmony with God's will, there will be no need of law; where love in its fullness will unite all hearts in praise of the goodness of the Father of us all." And he advised Emily's mother to "wait patiently" to rejoin her daughter. "The thin curtain of mortality only separates us from the love which shall be revealed." [19]

On Sunday morning, March 13, 1881, Captain Henry Hasbrouck of the Fourth Artillery, also of the West Point Class of 1861, saw Upton working in his office. Hasbrouck went in and asked him how he felt. Upton looked at him for a moment, then broke down. He laid his head on his desk and sobbed. Hasbrouck tried to comfort him and finally got him to walk back to his quarters. Upton told Hasbrouck that he had lost his will power and the respect of the other officers in the regiment, that his tactical system was a failure, especially his method of deploying skirmishers, and that if the United States continued to use it the next war would be disastrous. His tactics could not be adjusted to companies of over 100 men and his professional reputation was ruined. Finally exhausted, Upton fell into a fitful sleep.

On Monday he went about his ordinary duties. That night Hasbrouck visited him, and again found him depressed. Hasbrouck induced him to talk about a proposed visit to Monterey, and Upton took enough interest in the subject to ask when the trains departed on Tuesday. Then Upton said he had to finish a letter and Hasbrouck left.

Upton wrote to Sara that he was distressed over his tactics because "it has seemed to me that I must give up my system and lose my military reputation." He did not know how it would all end, but hoped that God would "lead me to sacrifice myself, rather than to perpetuate a method which might in the future cost a single man his life." He asked Sara for her prayers. He began to tell her of a visit to Oakland and to describe the scenery there, then abruptly ended the letter. "I don't feel like writing any more. Only let me feel that I have your love and sympathy."

After sealing the letter to Sara, he began to write the Adjutant General of the United States. "In my effort to revise the tactics so that they might apply to companies over two hundred strong," he said, "I discovered that the double column and the deployment by numbers, when compared with the French method, was a failure." After a pause, he continued, "The fours, too, I was forced to admit . . ." but he could go no further. He dropped the pen and put his hand to his throbbing head. Finally he picked up the pen again and began another note to the Adjutant General. "Sir: I hereby tender my resignation as colonel of the Fourth Artillery."

He signed his resignation, "Very respectfully, Emory Upton, Colonel, 4th Artillery," and placed it in the middle of his desk. Then he picked up his Colt .45 pistol and shot himself through the head.[20]

At 6:30 on Tuesday morning, March 15, 1881, Ah Sing, Upton's Chinese servant, entered Upton's room, made a fire, and cleaned and polished the colonel's boots. He saw Upton slumped over his desk and, thinking he was asleep, did not disturb him. At 8 A.M. the cook sent Ah Sing back to call the colonel for breakfast. When he tried to wake him, the servant saw the pistol on the desk and blood around Upton's head. Ah Sing ran from the room and found Captain Hasbrouck who rushed back to Upton's room, saw what had happened, and informed General McDowell. The Departmental commander sent a telegram to the War Department, and the news quickly spread throughout the army.[21]

On the afternoon of March 19 the men of the Fourth Artillery escorted Upton's body, which had been embalmed and placed in a hermetically sealed metallic casket, to Van Ness Avenue in San Francisco. There the Second Brigade of the California National Guard met and replaced the regulars as the escort. General McDowell and other California officers served as pallbearers. All along the line of march flags hung from the buildings at half-mast, and the streets were crowded with observers. The Guardsmen escorted the body to the Washington Street wharf, where Upton's remains were placed on the tugboat *General McPherson*. The next day the corpse was shipped east with two junior officers as guards.

General Richard Arnold arranged the funeral, which took place on March 29 in Auburn, New York. Services were held on the banks of Lake Owasco in the chapel of Sand Beach Church, where Upton had been married. Sherman, Wilson, Du Pont, Professor Peter S. Michie of West Point, General Alexander, Adjutant General Frederick Townsend, and General John C. Tidball served as pallbearers. Many other officers, all in full-dress uniform, attended. They buried Upton next to Emily in the Sand Beach Cemetery.[22]

Upton's will was a short document. He held 280 shares of stock in the Upton Manufacturing Company, an agricultural implement firm owned by his brother James, which he divided among his four sisters. He bequeathed $500 to each of his four older brothers and $1,200 to his younger brother. Upton gave his nephew Emory Upton Alexander $1,000 and his niece Katie Upton $500. His personal effects went to his parents. The royalties from his *Tactics* would be Sara's. Finally, he gave his sword to his brother James, to be given to the first nephew or collateral relation by the name of Upton who graduated from West Point and entered the army.[23]

For weeks after Upton's suicide army men speculated on its cause. "What could it have been?" Wilson cried. "I was never more astounded in my life." He could think of no adequate explanation. It certainly could not have been because of Emily, dead now for over a decade, and Upton's headaches did not constitute sufficient cause for "such a man" to commit "such an act."[24]

Everyone who had known Upton was asking the same question. His sister Sara said, "His sad death is a great sorrow to me and it will always be shrouded in mystery."[25] Church, in the *Army and Naval Journal*, provided one explanation. "If officers of the Army had been asked to select from their number the man who was least likely to come to a violent end by his own hand," Church began, "those who know him would have been as apt to select Emory Upton as any one of the entire list." Upton was universally regarded as "one of fortune's favorites" and was one of the best known officers in the army. His grief over his dead wife was one possible cause of his suicide, but it could not have been the only motive. "Upton was a man of excitable nature," Church pointed out, "who showed a certain intensity of energy which led him into a good deal of worry when he did not see the way directly to the accomplishment of an object." Drawing upon his long acquaintance with him, Church declared that Upton "would fret himself sometimes under such circumstances as a man would who found himself in a *cul de sac* with an invincible determination to push ahead." This disposition, aggravated by his headaches, may have caused Upton's suicide.[26] Church was saying, politely, that Upton could not live with what he considered to be failure.

Influence

"I think Upton was the most conscientious man and the finest, and the most up-right one I ever knew. And we both know that he was as brave and as good a soldier as ever lived." James H. Wilson to Henry du Pont, March 16, 1881.

One thing remained—the manuscript of "The Military Policy of the United States." Upton's suicide had sent a thrill of horror through the army and increased his already great prominence. Army men began to think of him as one of the most promising and heroic of American officers, a man who might have reached unknown heights but for his physical disability. Still he had left behind a manuscript, and professional soldiers began to demand that it be published.

The manuscript was in the possession of Henry du Pont. Just before he committed suicide, Upton had told his sister Sara that if anything happened to him he wanted Du Pont to finish the work. At the funeral, Sara talked to Du Pont about the manuscript, and he promised that as soon as possible he would complete and publish it.[1]

But Du Pont's obligations as a member of E. I. du Pont and Company and as president and manager of the Wilmington and Northern Railroad kept him from the work. Meanwhile Peter S. Michie, professor of natural philosophy at West Point and an 1863 graduate of the Academy, was writing a memoir of Upton. Du Pont lent Michie some of his correspondence with Upton and sent him the military policy manuscript. Michie also borrowed correspondence from Sherman, Wilson, and Upton's brothers and sisters. Michie's *Life and Letters of Emory Upton* appeared in 1885. Michie told the story of Upton's life in a clear, straightforward manner, quoting copiously—and without editing— from Upton's letters. The result was an excellent volume.

In his book, Michie summarized Upton's military policy manuscript. He was impressed with the work and he urged Du Pont to publish it simultaneously with his own *Upton*. Michie felt the major service of his own book would be to "excite enough interest in the Military Policy to make people buy it when it appears." [2] But Du Pont still could not find the necessary time to complete the manuscript. Michie, Sherman, Wilson, Schofield, and other officers pressed him to publish it, but Du Pont felt that the manuscript needed some polishing and that a brief discussion of the last three years of the Civil War should be included. A sensitive man, Du Pont felt guilty about disappointing Upton's friends. He hinted to Sara that he would like to give the manuscript to someone else for completion. Sara agreed that the work should not be published "until in a perfect condition," but refused to allow Du Pont to give it to someone else. She told him, "I should feel as if it would be a betrayal of trust to have anyone else finish it." [3]

Late in 1885 William W. Appleton, Upton's publisher, tried to prod Du Pont into more activity. He wanted to take advantage of the stir created by Michie's book, which he had also published, and feared that if they waited much longer the interest in the manuscript which Michie's summary had aroused would diminish. Appleton and Du Pont had a meeting to discuss publication, but nothing came of it.[4]

By now the General-in-chief had lost patience. Sherman told Michie that Du Pont "should immediately publish Upton's Chapters on the Military Policy without one word of endorsement or comment." If Du Pont did not, Sherman added, "I for one will question his fidelity to the friend who trusted him as a brother."

The General-in-chief explained that the world was like a kaleidoscope—after the tube was turned, the former figures were lost to the vision and soon to the memory. He determined that this should not happen to Upton. Mankind, Sherman said, paid the penalty of the neglects of its ancestors of hundreds of years past, "but if by prudence and foresight we can lessen the burdens of our children and grandchildren, we should do it." Upton had shown that "by clinging to old prejudices, we have entailed on our children and grandchildren a burden impossible for them to bear." The only hope was for America to adopt a more sensible military policy. "The least we can do is to show them the way out of the scrape," which the publication of Upton's work would do. Finally, Sherman summarized his feelings toward the man he had respected and loved. "Thoughts are ephemeral. Deeds substantial. To unite both requires genius." [5]

But even Sherman's wrath was not enough. Du Pont refused to publish the manuscript until it was complete. He worked on it when he could, but his business duties took most of his time. Sara occasionally asked about his progress, but after her marriage in 1887 she lost interest.[6] Du Pont did circulate the manuscript among a select group of army officers, but he never completed it.

Meanwhile the army struggled through its dark ages. Congress and the public paid it little if any attention. There was a ripple of internal reform, but nothing of importance was done. The army had become a useless organization. It was designed to fight Indians and there were no Indians left for it to fight. It was incapable of waging a major war against a well-prepared and determined opponent, and nothing had been done to make the militia capable of fighting such a war. As Sherman had feared, Upton and his warnings were forgotten.

Then, in 1898, America went to war. Luckily, her opponent was neither well prepared nor determined, else the result might have been catastrophe. The 28,000 officers and men of the army were scattered over the country, usually in detachments of less than a company in size. No general staff, or any other agency, existed to plan for mobilization, organization, and training. No provision had been made for assembling or transporting an overseas expedition, or for the handling of large bodies of troops. Except for some aged Civil War veterans, no officer in the army had ever seen a force larger than a regiment, and few had seen even that much. The National Guard, or the organized militia of the states, numbered something over 100,000 in size, but except for some knowledge of close-order infantry drill the Guardsmen were innocent of any understanding of the military art. Further, the Guard was, like the old militia, under the control of the governors of the sovereign states. The War Department tried to impose some measure of control over the Guard, but the "militia interest" forced it to accept a bill which obligated the President to accept bodily any National Guard regiment offered at full strength. No West Pointers, or other regular army personnel, could be appointed to the Guard regiments.[7]

Thanks to the hearty cooperation of the Spanish, the United States won her war. But she did so at immense, unnecessary cost. In Cuba, in July, American soldiers fought in the old, heavy wool uniforms of the Civil War. They fired a black-powder cartridge which every other civilized nation in the world had discarded in favor of smokeless powder. Due to the inefficiency of the staff bureaus, the troops ate rancid meat and suffered terribly from typhoid and malaria. When it was all over an enraged public demanded a scapegoat, and Secretary of War Russell Alger lost his position.

Elihu Root replaced Alger. His charge was to still criticism of the administration, administer the new colonies, and, possibly, to find an adequate military policy for the United States. Hard-working and sincere, Root took his task seriously. Shocked at what the Spanish War had revealed, he undertook to reform the army and to find a workable reserve system for it.

Shortly after his appointment, Root had a talk with young Major William H. Carter, who had served under Upton in the seventies. Carter told Root of *The Armies of Asia and Europe,* and later found a copy in a secondhand bookstore in Washington. He sent the book to Root, who read it and then Michie's biography. Intrigued by Upton's ideas, Root began a search for the military policy manuscript. Henry du Pont, by now a Senator from Delaware, produced it, and Root put two young officers to work on it.[8] They made few changes. They eliminated a chapter on "Command and Administration," covering the controversies between Winfield Scott as General-in-chief and Jefferson Davis as Secretary of War, and one on Roman military policy. The editors also deleted introductory paragraphs to some of the chapters which they considered repetitious. Otherwise the manuscript remained intact.[9]

In January, 1904, the War Department published *The Military Policy of the United States.* Root sent copies to thirty-three newspaper and magazine editors. The Secretary had become Upton's chief follower, and his program of reform for the army was based on Upton's recommendations. He later said that Upton's writings "gave me the detail on which I could base recommendations and overcome my ignorance as a civilian." He hoped the *Military Policy* would create support for his program, and it did.[10]

The Root reforms contained most of Upton's specific proposals. Root began his legislative campaign by declaring that "the real object of having an Army is to provide for war, . . . yet the precise contrary is . . . the theory upon which the entire treatment of our Army proceeded for the thirty-three year period between the Civil War and the war with Spain." He believed that his own office should control the army, but through a single chief of staff and not through the various staff bureaus. He told Congress, "I do not want to relieve the Secretary of War of responsibility, but I want you to enable him to discharge this responsibility, through a military officer who will gather together in the performance of staff duties all the considerations affecting the decision that the Secretary has to make, and do it with military knowledge."

The principal features of Root's reforms included an enlarged federal army, closer federal supervision of the National Guard, an elaborate system of education for army officers, the three-battalion regiment, interchangeable service in the staff and line, and the establishment of a general staff. But Root ignored Upton's key proposals—for the National Volunteers as the chief reserve system and for the independence of the army and its monopoly over the armed forces of the nation.[11]

The *Military Policy* continued to be used by those who wished to change the American military system. Before 1916 Upton's book went through four printings, all sponsored by the War Department. In 1914, during the Mexican Revolution, the House of Representatives published the chapters bearing on the Mexican War, and in 1916 the book appeared in an abridged form with an introduction by General Hugh L. Scott. Finally, in 1941, Senator Carl Hayden sponsored the publication of "Evil Effects of Short-Term Army Enlistments: Extracts from *The Military Policy of the United States* by Emory Upton." All together, the government sold 12,227 copies of the book in one form or another and distributed countless others free.[12]

In 1916 Upton's spirit hovered over the Congressional hearings on national defense. Nearly every witness either mentioned him or discussed his ideas. In his introduction to the epitome of the *Military Policy,* which the army published that year, Chief of Staff Scott declared that his purpose was "to bring to the attention of our citizens the facts of our military history as bearing upon the present problem of national preparedness for defense." Woodrow Wilson's Secretary of War, Lindley M. Garrison, spoke of Upton as a "great military authority," and Assistant Secretary of War Henry Breckinridge praised Upton as "the greatest military philosopher who has ever written in this country." [13]

The leaders of the American army in 1916 belonged to a generation of professional soldiers which had been brought up on Emory Upton. They were familiar with Upton's ideas and supporters of his program. In 1905 the topic for the Military Service Institution's essay competition was "How Far Does Democracy Affect the Organization and Discipline of our Armies, and How Can its Influence be Most Effectually Utilized?" Colonel James S. Pettit won the contest with a paper which was a summary of the *Military Policy.* Pettit said of Upton's book, "A careful reading of its pages will give a complete answer to the title of our essay." [14] Even General Leonard Wood, a non-West Pointer and therefore in many ways outside the main stream of professionalism, was an admirer of Upton. In his *Our Military History,* published in 1916 to influence legislation, Wood summarized Upton's arguments, seconded his conclusions, and roundly declared that "every American should read" Upton's work.[15]

In the preparedness crisis of 1916, the general staff and Secretary Garrison sponsored a plan that in its essential

points was a copy of Upton's National Volunteer scheme.
They asked for a regular army of 281,000 men with enough
reserves to raise it to 500,000, plus a "Continental Army" of
part-time trainees. The Continental Army was to be a
federal rather than a state force, secured through volunteering. It would number 500,000 men. The Uptonians did
not win a complete victory, but they did secure significant
gains. The National Defense Act of 1916 retained the Guard
as the principal reserve, which prompted Secretary Garrison
to resign in disgust, but the bill did impose more federal
control over the Guard, and it opened the way for a national
army to be raised by conscription and organized by the
federal government. The American army which fought World
War I was organized in large measure in accordance with
Upton's ideas. By the second decade of the twentieth century most of the reforms for which Upton struggled, and
which he despaired of ever achieving, were realities.[16]

But the ultimate system for which Upton worked did not
prevail. The American army never completely freed itself
from civilian control nor did it ever achieve a monopoly on
armed force within the United States. Its principal reserve
continued to be the National Guard regiments, and those
organizations still retained their state orientation. No longer
was the army neglected or despised, but neither did it become a state within the state. It remained an agency subordinate to, and controlled by, civilians.

In the struggles of 1917–18 and 1941–45 the army did
a magnificent job. In part, this was due to Upton's influence.
His demands for internal army reform helped give the
United States a modern armed force. His attempts to find
an adequate reserve system for the army and his criticism of
the militia provided a starting point for intelligent discussion
and contributed to a satisfactory compromise.

Perhaps more important Upton, who was proud of his
profession, helped keep alive a sense of pride and purpose

in an army that might otherwise have sunk into a permanent morass. He was a devoted public servant who strove to anticipate and meet his nation's needs. At times his vision was narrow, but his contributions were real. When he killed himself he was certain he was a failure. He was wrong. Emory Upton both symbolized and helped preserve the best in the army.

Notes

Chapter I

1 James Harrison Wilson, in the introduction to Peter S. Michie, *The Life and Letters of Emory Upton* (New York, 1885).

2 Merritt Starr, "General Emory Upton—His Brothers, His Career," *Oberlin Alumni Magazine* (May, 1922), 12–14; Michie, *Upton*, 1–3.

3 James Harris Fairchild, *Oberlin, the Colony and the College* (Oberlin, 1883), 11–53; Starr, "Upton," *Oberlin Alumni Magazine*, 14; Allen Johnson and Dumas Malone (eds.), *Dictionary of American Biography* (New York, 1931), VI, 394–95; Robert S. Fletcher, *A History of Oberlin College* (Oberlin, 1943), II, 665–87.

4 Starr, "Upton," *Oberlin Alumni Magazine*, 14.

5 Michie, *Upton*, 3–9.

6 Henry du Pont to his mother, June 23, 1856, Henry Algernon du Pont papers in the Henry Francis du Pont Winterthur Manuscripts, Eleutherian Mills Historical Library, Wilmington, Delaware. All Du Pont letters cited in this work are printed with the permission of the Eleutherian Mills Historical Library. The collection will hereinafter be cited as Du Pont Papers.

7 See Du Pont's letters to his parents for the period 1856–61, Du Pont Papers; Sidney Forman, *West Point: A History of the United States Military Academy* (New York, 1950), 36–74; R. Ernest Dupuy, *Where They Have Trod: The West Point Tradition in American Life* (New York, 1940), 8–183.

8 Du Pont to his mother, July 14, 1856, Du Pont Papers.

9 Michie, *Upton*, 12.

10 Du Pont to his mother, September 14, 1856, Du Pont Papers. Scott's cockade was nonregulation.

11 Michie, *Upton*, 23.

12 *Ibid.*, 12.

13 Henry Wager Halleck, *Elements of Military Art and Science* (2nd ed.; New York, 1862).

14 Du Pont to Mother, September 14, 1856, Du Pont Papers.
15 Michie, *Upton*, 13–24.
16 Morris Schaff, *The Spirit of Old West Point*, 1858–1862 (Boston, 1907), 142–48; Wilson's introduction to Michie, *Upton*.
17 Michie, *Upton*, 29.
18 *Ibid.*, 31–33.
19 *Ibid.*, 33–34.
20 Michie, *Upton*, 34; Du Pont to his father, April 14, 1861, Du Pont Papers.
21 Du Pont discusses the possibilities in a letter to his father, April 28, 1861, Du Pont Papers.

Chapter ii

1 James Harrison Wilson, *Under the Old Flag* (New York, 1912), I, 181.
2 Michie, *Upton*, 42.
3 Emory Upton, *The Military Policy of the United States* (Washington, 1904), 42.
4 *The War of the Rebellion: A Compilation of the Official Records of the Union and Confederate Armies* (Washington, 1880–1901), Series I, Vol. II, 350–51, cited hereinafter as *Official Records* (unless otherwise indicated all citations are to Series I). Michie, *Upton*, 42–51.
5 *Official Records*, XI, Pt. 1, pp. 618–22; Michie, *Upton*, 51–59.
6 Richard Barry, "Emory Upton, Military Genius," New York *Times Magazine* (June 16, 1918); Michie, *Upton*, 63–67; Isaac O. Best, *History of the 121st New York State Infantry* (Chicago, 1921), 28.
7 Best, *121st New York*, 28–51.
8 *Official Records*, XXVII, Pt. 1, p. 673; Best, *121st New York*, 42–79.
9 *Official Records*, XXVII, Pt. 1, p. 673; Best, *121st New York*, 84–91; Michie, *Upton*, 75.
10 *Official Records*, XXIX, Pt. 1, pp. 587–89, 592–93; Best, *121st New York*, 99–103; Michie, *Upton*, 83–85.
11 Michie, *Upton*, 76–91.
12 All letters and recommendations are in the "Appointment, Commission, and Personnel File of Major General Emory

Upton," Records of the War Department: The Adjutant General's Office, National Archives, Washington, D. C.

13 Upton to Du Pont, March 6, 1879, Du Pont Papers.

14 A. F. Becke, *An Introduction to the History of Tactics, 1740–1905* (London, 1909), 57–108; Robert S. Quimby, *The Background of Napoleonic Warfare, the Theory of Military Tactics in Eighteenth Century France* (New York, 1957), 308–14.

15 George T. Stevens, *Three Years in the Sixth Corps* (Albany, New York, 1866), 331–32.

16 Best, *121st New York*, 127–36; *Official Records*, XXXVI, Pt. 1, pp. 67, 665–71.

17 Best, *121st New York*, 138–39; Michie, *Upton*, 116.

18 Bruce Catton, *A Stillness at Appomattox* (Garden City, New York, 1954), 125–26; *Official Records*, XXXVI, Pt. 1, pp. 665–71; Best, *121st New York*, 141–45.

19 Best, *121st New York*, 152–63; *Official Records*, XXXVI, Pt. 1, pp. 70, 665–71.

20 *Official Records*, XXXVI, Pt. 1, pp. 670–73; Theodore F. Vaill, *History of the Second Connecticut Volunteer Heavy Infantry* (Winsted, Connecticut, 1868), 61–67.

21 Michie, *Upton*, 108–109, 123.

22 *Official Records*, XL, Pt. 1, p. 492; Michie, *Upton*, 116.

23 Michie, *Upton*, 122.

Chapter III

1 Wilson, *Under the Old Flag*, I, 554; Michie, *Upton*, xxiii, 125; *Official Records*, XL, Pt. 1, p. 492, and XLIII, Pt. 1, pp. 162–64; 173, and Pt. 2, pp. 119, 199; P. H. Sheridan, *Personal Memoirs* (New York, 1888), II, 27–30.

2 Michie, *Upton*, 123.

3 E. N. Gilpin Diary, December, 1864, Journals and Diaries of E. N. Gilpin, Library of Congress, Washington, D. C.

4 Wilson, *Under the Old Flag*, I, 553; *Official Records*, XLIII, Pt. 2, pp. 630, 637, and XLV, Pt. 2, pp. 171, 173, and XLIX, Pt. 1, p. 598, and Pt. 2, p. 663; Michie, *Upton*, xv, 130–43.

5 Wilson, *Under the Old Flag*, II, 207; *Official Records*, XLIX, Pt. 1., pp. 471–72, and Pt. 2, pp. 11, 136–37.

6 Michie, *Upton*, 157; Wilson, *Under the Old Flag*, II, 221–30.

7   Gilpin Diary, April 10, 1865, Journals and Diaries of E. N. Gilpin.
8   *Official Records*, XLIX, Pt. 1, pp. 471–74; Michie, *Upton*, 159; Wilson, *Under the Old Flag*, II, 258–65.
9   *Official Records*, XLIX, Pt. 2, pp. 601–604.
10 *Ibid.*, 617–18, 633–34, 665–66.
11 *Ibid.*, 685; Best, *121st New York*, 241.
12 *Official Records*, XLIX, Pt. 2, pp. 749–50, 789, 802, 817.
13 Michie, *Upton*, 174.
14 *Official Records*, XLIX, Pt. 1, p. 478.
15 Wilson, *Under the Old Flag*, II, 274–75.
16 Michie, *Upton*, xvi.
17 Letter to Gilpin, June 6, 1878, Journals and Diaries of E. N. Gilpin.
18 See Wilson's introduction to Michie, *Upton*.

Chapter iv

1   Michie, *Upton*, 178.
2   Barry, "Upton," New York *Times Magazine* (June 16, 1918 [an interview with Wilson]).
3   Michie, *Upton*, 181–86.
4   *Official Records*, LXVIII, Pt. 2, p. 1204.
5   Michie, *Upton*, 187–88.
6   Richard A. Preston, Sydney F. Wise, and Herman O. Werner, *Men in Arms: A History of Warfare and its Interrelationships with Western Society* (New York, 1956), 136–38.
7   *Ibid.*, 176–95; Becke, *Introduction to History of Tactics*, 18, 72.
8   Theodore Ropp, *War in the Modern World* (New York, 1962), 162.
9   Becke, *History of Tactics*, 40.
10 The American army was trying to accommodate. Silas Casey, in his work on tactics, declared, "The revolution which has been wrought within a few years past in the weapons both of artillery and infantry, has necessitated a departure from those processional movements and formation in order of battle, which characterized the school of Frederick the Great." But his innovations were hardly sufficient to meet the need; Casey recommended two ranks instead of three and a faster marching pace. Silas Casey, *Infantry Tactics . . .* (New York, 1862), I, 5–6.

11   Preston, Wise, and Werner, *Men in Arms*, 245; John K. Mahon, "Civil War Infantry Assault Tactics," *Military Affairs*, XXV (1961), 59.

12   Jay Luvaas, *The Military Legacy of the Civil War: The European Inheritance* (Chicago, 1959), 106.

13   Gilpin Diary, entry of April 26, 1865, Journals and Diaries of E. N. Gilpin.

14   For a discussion of French tactics, see Quimby, *The Background of Napoleonic Warfare;* Michie, *Upton,* 191–93; William Addleman Ganoe, *The History of the United States Army* (New York, 1942), 317.

15   Michie, *Upton,* 189–96.

16   Upton to Du Pont, August 9, 1866, Du Pont Papers.

17   Emory Upton, *Infantry Tactics: Double and Single Rank. Adapted to American Topography and Improved Fire-arms* (New York, 1875), ii–iv; Michie, *Upton,* 197–212.

18   Upton, *Tactics,* 9–73; Casey, *Infantry Tactics,* I, 22–98.

19   Upton, *Tactics,* vii–viii.

20   Upton later confirmed his impressions in a conversation with Sherman. Upton to Sherman, November 8, 1867, William T. Sherman Papers, Library of Congress.

21   Emory Upton, *A New System of Infantry Tactics: Double and Single Rank. Adapted to American Topography and Improved Fire-arms* (New York, 1873), 117, 270–71; Emory Upton, *The Armies of Asia and Europe* (New York, 1878), 299–301; Charles J. Ardant du Picq, *Battle Studies,* trans. by Col. John N. Greely and Maj. Robert C. Cotton from 8th edition (Harrisburg, Penn., 1958), xvi, 193, 250–53.

22   *The Army and Navy Journal,* February 2, 1867, September 5, 1868, May 22, 1869, November 19, 1870.

23   Donald Nevius Bigelow, *William Conant Church and the Army and Navy Journal* (New York, 1952), 125.

24   Michie, *Upton,* 217–41.

25   Upton to Wilson, November 21, 1867, James Harrison Wilson Papers, Library of Congress.

26   Michie, *Upton,* 220–36.

27   Upton to Wilson, December 4, 1868, Wilson Papers.

28   Upton to Wilson, August 30, 1868, Wilson Papers.

29   Upton to Wilson, October 15, 1868, Wilson Papers.

30   Upton to Wilson, December 12, 1868, Wilson Papers.

31   Upton to Wilson, May 15, 1869, Wilson Papers.

32 Upton to T. A. Jenckes, January 14, 1869, Thomas A. Jenckes Papers, Library of Congress.
33 Michie, *Upton*, 235–41.

Chapter v

1   Michie, *Upton*, 243–45.
2   *Ibid.*, 246–51; Forman, *West Point*, 153; Hugh T. Reed, *Cadet Life at West Point* (Chicago, 1896), 232.
3   Michie, *Upton*, 275–78.
4   *Ibid.*, 257–71; Upton to Wilson, February 20, 1871, Wilson Papers; Belknap to Church, March 26, 1871, William C. Church Papers, Library of Congress.
5   Upton to Du Pont, April 7, 1871, Du Pont Papers.
6   Upton to Du Pont, January 18 and December 22, 1872, Du Pont Papers.
7   *Times* (New York), March 3–5, 1873; Upton to Du Pont, March 7, 1873, Du Pont Papers; Reed, *Cadet Life*, 227.
8   Upton to Sherman, May 29, 1875, Sherman Papers.
9   Upton to Wilson, May 29, 1874, Wilson Papers.
10 Upton to Du Pont, June 30, 1870, Du Pont Papers.
11 Upton to Du Pont, March 15, 1871, Du Pont Papers.
12 Upton, *Infantry Tactics* (3rd [1875] ed.), vii.
13 See the Sherman-Upton correspondence in the Sherman Papers for 1872–73; Upton to Du Pont, December 17, 1872, Du Pont Papers.
14 Michie, *Upton*, 207.
15 Upton to Du Pont, December 28, 1872, Du Pont Papers.
16 Du Pont to Father, January 26, 1873, Du Pont Papers.
17 Du Pont to Mother, September 6, 1857, Du Pont Papers.
18 Upton to Du Pont, March 1, 1873, Du Pont Papers.
19 Upton to Du Pont, March 13, 1873, Du Pont Papers.
20 Upton to Du Pont, June 19, 1873, Du Pont Papers.
21 Upton to Du Pont, July 18, 1873, Du Pont Papers.
22 Upton to Du Pont, August 12, 1873, Du Pont Papers.
23 Upton to Du Pont, August 23, 1873, Du Pont Papers; *Army and Navy Journal*, December 6, 1873.
24 Upton, *A New System of Infantry Tactics*.
25 *Cavalry Tactics, United States Army, Assimilated to the Tactics of Infantry and Artillery* (New York, 1874); *Artillery Tactics, United States Army, Assimilated to the Tactics of Infantry and Cavalry* (New York, 1875).

26 Upton to Du Pont, October 31, 1874, Du Pont Papers.
27 Upton to Du Pont, November 23, 1874, Du Pont Papers.
28 Upton to Du Pont, February 25, 1875, Du Pont Papers.
29 Upton to Church, October 28, 1874, Church Papers.
30 Upton to Church, March 7, 1874, Du Pont Papers.
31 *Army and Navy Journal*, August 2 and 23, 1873, March 14, 1874.
32 *Army and Navy Journal*, September 18, 1869.
33 *Army and Navy Journal*, November 19, 1870.
34 *Army and Navy Journal*, April 4, July 4 and 11, 1874.
35 Upton to Wilson, May 4, 1874, Wilson Papers.
36 Upton to Church, April 7, 1874, Church Papers. Church and other American traditionalists were not alone. Du Picq, for example, was weakest in his discussion of cavalry in modern war. *Battle Studies*, 179–204.
37 Ganoe, *The History of the United States Army*, 360.
38 Michie, *Upton*, 216–17.
39 The first edition appeared in 1867, the second in 1873, and the third in 1875. In 1891 Appleton and Company reprinted the 1875 edition.
40 Sara Upton to Du Pont, February 28, 1883, Du Pont Papers.
41 Michael Howard, *The Franco-Prussian War: The German Invasion of France, 1870–1871* (New York, 1962), 103.
42 The Thayer Club liked the paper so much that it ordered it printed—the first to receive such an honor. "I felt greatly gratified," Upton told Du Pont. To Du Pont, October 31, 1874, Du Pont Papers. In saying that he disapproved of flowing around the flanks of strong points, Upton was for one of the few times in his life mistaken about tactical developments. Upton later published the paper as "The Prussian Company Column," in the *International Review* (March, 1875), 302–16.

Chapter VI

1 B. H. Liddell Hart, *Sherman, Soldier, Realist, American* (New York, 1958), 416–17; Michie, *Upton*, 284–86; Barry, "Upton," New York *Times Magazine* (June 16, 1918), 12; Sherman to Belknap, August 17, 1870, Sherman Papers.
2 See Upton to Sherman, February 5, 1868, Sherman Papers.
3 Upton, *The Armies of Asia and Europe*, iii–ix; Upton to Du Pont, October 31, 1874, Du Pont Papers.

4   Michie, *Upton,* 290–98, 341; Upton to Du Pont, June 27, 1875, Du Pont Papers.
5   Upton, *Armies of Asia,* iii–ix.
6   Michie, *Upton,* 314, 373, 378.
7   Gordon A. Craig, *The Politics of the Prussian Army, 1640–1945* (New York, 1956), 140–46; Alfred Vagts, *A History of Militarism: Civilian and Military* (rev. ed.; New York, 1959), 191–93; Howard, *Franco-Prussian War,* 19–20; Upton, *Armies of Asia,* 201–203; Walter Goerlitz, *History of the German General Staff 1657–1945* (New York 1953), 69–103; Eugène Carrias, *L'Armeé allemande. Son histoire, son organization, son tactique* (Paris, 1938).
8   Spenser Wilkinson, *The Brain of an Army: A Popular Account of the German General Staff* (Westminster, England, 1895), 76–83; Vagts, *Militarism,* 200–205; Craig, *Prussian Army,* xv–xvi; Goerlitz, *German General Staff,* 66–99; Bismarck retained the power to override the General Staff when it injected itself into problems he considered not to belong to it, even though the staff might consider those problems to be military ones. Ropp, *War in the Modern World,* 179.
9   Wilkinson, *Brain of an Army,* 102.
10 Howard, *Franco-Prussian War,* 13–14, 37–38; Vagts, *Militarism,* 209.
11 Vagts, *Militarism,* 225–26; Wilkinson, *Brain of an Army,* 21.
12 Michie, *Upton,* 378–79, 387–91, 416–19; Upton to Du Pont, April 1 and September 30, 1877, January 13, 1878, Du Pont Papers.
13 Upton to Sherman, November 22, 1877, Sherman Papers; Upton to Wilson, February 2, 1878, Wilson Papers; Sherman to Upton, February 9, 1878, Sherman Papers.
14 Upton, *Armies of Asia,* introduction; Richard Brown, "General Emory Upton—The Army's Mahan," *Military Affairs,* XVII (1953), 126; Upton to Greene, January 25, 1879. F. V. Greene Papers, New York Public Library.
15 Upton, *Armies of Asia* 12–86.
16 *Ibid.,* 96–97.
17 *Ibid.,* 98–317; *passim;* John W. Hacket, *The Profession of Arms* (London, 1962), 38.
18 Upton, *Armies of Asia,* 317–23, 369.
19 *Ibid.,* 320–24, 337–53. Some authorities have found the origins

of Upton's idea in John C. Calhoun's proposal, made while
he was Secretary of War, for an expansive army. Calhoun
did propose such a plan—based on reducing the number of
privates in a company during peacetime—and Upton later
praised him for it, but nevertheless Upton's expansive army
plan came from his investigation in Germany, not from Calhoun. Upton did not even know much about Calhoun's proposal until 1878 when he began research on the military
policy of the United States. Upton, *Military Policy*, 149–51;
Margaret L. Coit, *John C. Calhoun: American Portrait*
(Boston, 1950), 129.

20 Upton, *Armies of Asia*, 327–29; T. Harry Williams, *Americans
    at War: The Development of the American Military System*
    (Baton Rouge, 1960), 105–24.
21 Upton, *Armies of Asia*, 366.
22 *Ibid.*, 141.
23 *Ibid.*, 367.
24 *Ibid.*, 369.
25 Upton to Garfield, June 6 and July 24, 1878, James A Gar-
    field Papers, Library of Congress; Michie, *Upton*, 450–53.
    To Church, Upton confessed that the one task remaining
    to the militia was preserving law and order. Upton's pro-
    posals, after the appearance of his report, had been criticized
    by a letter writer to the *Army and Navy Journal* as an under-
    handed attempt to destroy the militia; Upton, in angrily
    refuting the charge, pointed out that the militia was the
    instrument created by the Constitution to maintain internal
    order. Upton to Church, December 13, 1878, Church Papers.
    And on August 11, 1878, he explicitly told Wilson, referring
    to the strikes, "I don't fear any danger to our institutions."
    Wilson Papers.
26 Upton told Du Pont: "Should we have war with England
    ten or twenty years from now and begin it as we did the
    last one, with 50,000 regulars [England] could lay every
    one of our larger seacoast cities under contribution, and it
    would require two or three years to shake her off." Upton to
    Du Pont, April 11, 1878, Du Pont Papers.
27 For a discussion of this problem, see Samuel P. Huntington,
    "Equilibrium and Disequilibrium in American Military
    Policy," *Political Science Quarterly*, LXXVI (1961), 490–94,
    and Halleck, *Elements of Military Art and Science*.

28 Upton, *Armies of Asia*, 368–69.
29 Halleck, *Elements of Military Art and Science*, 147. For a
    further discussion, centering around Halleck's efforts to
    eliminate the politicians from military command during the
    Civil War, see Stephen E. Ambrose, *Halleck: Lincoln's Chief
    of Staff* (Baton Rouge, 1962), 204–208.
30 John A. Logan, *The Volunteer Soldier of America* (Chicago
    1887), 119–20.
31 For a further discussion, see Russell Weigley, *Towards an
    American Army: Military Thought from Washington to
    Marshall* (New York, 1962), 100–27.
32 Upton to Du Pont, June 20, 1878, Du Pont Papers.
33 See the *Army and Navy Journal* for the last half of 1878;
    Walter Millis, *Arms and Men: A Study in American Military
    History* (New York, 1956), 143–45.

Chapter vii

1 Ganoe, *History of the United States Army*, 334, 352–53; C.
   Joseph Bernardo and Eugene H. Bacon, *American Military
   Policy: Its Development Since 1775* (2nd ed.; Harrisburg,
   Penn., 1961), 239.
2 *Army and Navy Journal*, February 23, 1877.
3 *Army and Navy Journal*, March 16, 1878; "Our Military, Past
   and Future," *Atlantic Monthly*, XLIV (November, 1879),
   561–75.
4 Upton to Wilson, April 1, 1878, Wilson Papers. See also
   Upton to Schofield, July 28, 1877, John Schofield Papers,
   Library of Congress.
5 Theodore Clarke Smith, *The Life and Letters of James
   Abram Garfield* (New Haven, Conn., 1925), I, 421.
6 U. S. House of Representatives, *Army Organization*, House
   Report No. 33, 40 Cong., 3 Sess. (Washington, 1869).
7 U. S. House of Representatives, *Army-Staff Organization*,
   House Report No. 74, 42 Cong., 3 Sess. (Washington, 1873).
8 U. S. Senate, *Reorganization of the Army*, Senate Report No.
   555, Pt. 2, 45 Cong., 3 Sess. (Washington, 1879), 2–4, 78–79,
   199, 426.
9 *Army and Navy Journal*, December 19, 1878; Upton to Garfield, January 4, 1879, Garfield Papers; Upton to Du Pont,
   January 13, 1879, Du Pont Papers.
10 Upton to Garfield, May 6, 1878, Garfield Papers.

11 Upton to Garfield, June 26, 1878, Garfield Papers.
12 Upton, *Military Policy*, 74; Upton to Garfield, July 24, 1878, Garfield Papers.
13 Michie, *Upton*, 450–53.
14 Upton to Garfield, September 16, 1878, Garfield Papers.
15 Upton to Garfield, October 10, 1878, Garfield Papers.
16 Upton to Wilson, October 21, 1878, Wilson Papers.
17 Upton to Wilson, December 26, 1878, Wilson Papers.
18 Halleck, *Elements of Military Art and Science;* Halleck to Francis Lieber, April 15, 1863, and May 1, 1864, Francis Lieber Correspondence, Henry Huntington Library, San Marino, Califorina. For a further discussion, see Ambrose, *Halleck.*
19 Upton to Wilson, April 15, 1878, Wilson Papers; Upton to Du Pont, September 30, 1877, Du Pont Papers.
20 Upton to Du Pont, April 11, 1878, Du Pont Papers.
21 Upton to Du Pont, November 6, 1878, Du Pont Papers.
22 Upton to Du Pont, November 29, 1878, Du Pont Papers.
23 Upton to Du Pont, November 19, 1878, and March 7, 1879, Du Pont Papers.
24 Upton to Sherman, April 14 and November 6, 1879, Sherman Papers.
25 Upton to Du Pont, June 10 and 19, 1880, Du Pont Papers.
26 Upton, *Military Policy*, 428.
27 Upton frequently and bitterly commented on political influence in the Civil War, especially the broad powers over state volunteers which the governors retained. He never understood the necessities under which Lincoln operated, which forced him to appeal to the governors for aid and to give them something in return. See William B. Hesseltine, *Lincoln and the War Governors* (New York, 1948).
28 See Walter Millis, *Arms and Men*, 117–18.
29 Coit, *John C. Calhoun*, 129; Upton, *Military Policy*, vii–xv; Huntington, "Equilibrium and Disequilibrium in American Military Policy," *Political Science Quarterly*, 489.
30 Upton, *Military Policy*, 3–68; John M. Palmer, *America In Arms: The Experience of the United States with Military Organization* (New Haven, Conn., 1941), 112.
31 Upton would not have agreed; he felt the chapters on the Civil War much more important. See his correspondence with Sherman, Garfield, and Wilson.

32   Palmer, *America in Arms,* 110–11. See also R. M. Cheseldine, "Where Upton Made His Big Mistake," *Infantry Journal* (March, 1930), 279–88, and Elbridge Colby, "Elihu Root and the National Guard," *Military Affairs,* XXIII (1959), 31.

33   Frederick P. Todd, "Our National Guard: An Introduction to its History," *Military Affairs,* V (1941), 31.

34   Upton, *Military Policy,* 85. Upton told Du Pont that "the Confederate idea lies at the bottom of all our military legislation and . . . this evil must be exposed whenever possible." Upton to Du Pont, March 16, 1880, Du Pont Papers.

35   Upton, *Military Policy,* 111–42.

36   *Ibid.,* 222.

37   *Ibid.,* 259–61, 437–38.

38   *Ibid.,* 235. Stanton's latest biographers believe that his greatest failure was in not making an efficient use of the regular army, because he did not force regular officers into volunteer regiments. Benjamin P. Thomas and Harold M. Hyman, *Stanton: The Life and Times of Lincoln's Secretary of War* (New York, 1962), 365.

39   Upton, *Military Policy,* 275–469, *passim.* Upton's description of Confederate policy was inaccurate. There was much more state influence over the armed forces than he would admit —but he was trying to influence policy, not write history.

40   Marvin A. Kreidberg and Merton G. Henry, *History of Military Mobilization in the United States Army, 1775–1945* (Department of the Army, 1955), 143–44; Williston B. Palmer, *The Evolution of Military Policy in the United States* (Carlisle Barracks, Penn., 1946), 6–7, 143–44.

41   Upton to Sherman, June 26, 1880, Sherman Papers. See also Upton to Du Pont, June 21, 1880, Du Pont Papers.

42   Upton to Du Pont, October 31, 1879, Du Pont Papers.

43   Upton, *Military Policy,* 280–84, 350–405.

44   Upton to Du Pont, January 13, 1878, Du Pont Papers.

45   Upton to Du Pont, December 19, 1879, Du Pont Papers.

46   Upton to Garfield, December 19, 1879, Garfield Papers.

47   Upton, *Military Policy,* 305, 318.

48   Alvin Brown, *The Armor of Organization* (New York, 1953), 191–92, comments that "the wish to void fundamental law is not often so plainly expressed."

49   Luvaas, *Military Legacy of the Civil War,* 94, 120, 132, 145.

50   Goerlitz, *German General Staff,* 93.

51 Quoted in Lynn Montross, *War Through the Ages* (New York, 1946), 452.

Chapter VIII

1 Entry of June 6, 1878, Journals and Diaries of E. N. Gilpin.
2 Michie, *Upton*, 466; Upton to Du Pont, July 22, 1878, Du Pont Papers.
3 Upton to Du Pont, April 1, 1877, and July 7, 1880, Du Pont Papers.
4 Upton to Du Pont, September 30, 1877, Du Pont Papers.
5 Michie, *Upton*, 462; Upton, *Military Policy*, 344–62. President Chester A. Arthur remitted the sentence in 1882, and Porter was reappointed colonel in 1886 to rank from May, 1861, but without back pay. See Otto Eisenschiml, *The Celebrated Case of Fitz-John Porter: An American Dreyfus Affair* (New York, 1950).
6 Upton to Du Pont, October 13, 1879, Du Pont Papers.
7 Upton to Sherman, January 3, 1880; Sherman Papers.
8 Michie, *Upton* 466–73; Becke, *Tactics*, 48; *Army and Navy Journal*, April 16, 1881.
9 Upton to Du Pont, April 12, 1879, Du Pont Papers.
10 Upton to Du Pont, February 28, 1880, Du Pont Papers; Williston B. Palmer, *Evolution of Military Policy in the United States*, 6–7.
11 Michie, *Upton*, 475–80; Upton to Du Pont, July 6, and September 8, and 22, 1880, Du Pont Papers.
12 Upton to Church, August 18, 1879, February 27 and March 3, 1880, Church Papers. Upton also corresponded with other army officers about the problem. See Upton to Greene, December 11, 1877, F. V. Greene Papers.
13 Emory Upton, "Facts in Favor of Compulsory Retirement," *United Service Magazine* IV (March, 1880), 19–32; Upton to Du Pont, September 22, 1880, Du Pont Papers.
14 Upton to Church, March 3, 1880, Church Papers.
15 *Army and Navy Journal*, March 13, 1880.
16 *Army and Navy Journal*, March 6, 1880.
17 Upton to the Adjutant General, June 21, 1880, Upton Personnel File; Upton added that he would join the regiment at once if it went into the field.
18 Michie, *Upton*, 280; Upton to Du Pont, February 4, 1881, Du Pont Papers.

19 Michie, *Upton,* 280–83.
20 *Ibid.,* 475–504; *Evening Bulletin* (San Francisco), March 16, 1881.
21 *Evening Bulletin* (San Francisco) March 16, 1881. See telegrams in Upton Personnel File.
22 *Army and Navy Journal,* March 26, April 2, 1881; Arnold to Du Pont, March 20 and 24, 1881, and Wilson to Du Pont, March 25, 1881, all in Du Pont Papers.
23 Upton's last will and testament, Genesee County Courthouse, Batavia, New York.
24 Wilson to Du Pont, March 16, 1881, Du Pont Papers.
25 Sara Upton to Du Pont, June 9, 1881, Du Pont Papers.
26 *Army and Navy Journal,* March 19, 1881.

Chapter IX

1 Sara Upton to Du Pont, June 9, 1881, Du Pont Papers.
2 Michie, *Upton;* Michie to Du Pont, April 9 and 17, 1881, Du Pont Papers.
3 Sara Upton to Du Pont, May 6 and 16, 1884, Du Pont Papers.
4 Appleton to Du Pont, December 2, 1885, Du Pont Papers.
5 Sherman to Michie, December 2, 1885, Du Pont Papers.
6 Sara Upton to Du Pont, March 10, December 22, 1887, Du Pont Papers.
7 Walter Millis, *The Martial Spirit* (Cambridge, 1931), 152–57. Congress also allowed for the formation of a few regiments of U.S. Volunteers, somewhat along the lines of Upton's National Volunteers, although they did not have professional officers. Theodore Roosevelt's First U.S. Volunteer Cavalry, the "Rough Riders," was the best known.
8 William H. Carter, *Creation of American General Staff,* Senate Document 119, 68 Cong., 1 Sess. (Washington, 1924), 1–2, 15, 35. Carter also served on a board with Hasbrouck and Sanger.
9 The original manuscript, in Upton's handwriting, is in the Du Pont Papers.
10 Philip C. Jessup, *Elihu Root* (New York, 1938), I, 242–43.
11 Frederick Palmer, Newton D. Baker, *America At War* (New York, 1931), I, 66. Root indicated the reason he ignored the National Volunteers in a speech given while laying the cornerstone of the Army War College building in Washington in 1903, when he said of the *Military Policy,* "The work

was written from a purely military point of view, and in some parts shows a failure to appreciate difficulties arising from our form of government and the habits and opinions of our people with which civil government has necessarily to deal in its direction of the military arm." Reprinted in Upton, *Military Policy,* iv.

12 Brown, "Upton," *Military Affairs,* 128–29; Millis, *Arms and Men,* 139–40; Williams, *Americans at War,* 91–101.

13 U. S. Senate, *Preparedness for National Defense: Hearings Before the Committee on Military Affairs,* Senate Document, 64 Cong., 1 Sess. (Washington, 1961); U. S. House of Representatives, *Hearings Before the Committee on Military Affairs,* 64 Cong., 1 Sess. (Washington, 1916), I, 12, 43.

14 Russell Weigley, *Towards an American Army* (New York, 1962), 156.

15 Leonard Wood, *Our Military History: Its Facts and Fallacies* (Chicago, 1916), 19.

16 Weigley, *Towards an American Army,* 218–20.

Bibliographical Note

The period from the end of the Civil War to the beginning of the Spanish-American War was a crucial one for the United States Army. During those thirty-three years its appearance changed but little, its uniforms, arms, organization, and size remaining about the same; internally, however, there was much ferment, and the basis for a modern army was laid. Despite this, the period has been virtually ignored; no serious study of Upton has been undertaken since 1885, while the post-Civil War careers of Schofield, Hancock, Sherman, and Sheridan—to mention a few of the more important army officers—have been neglected. There is room for much to be done, and no adequate history of the United States Army can be written until this work is done.

Physical Remains

The Genesee County Land Office in Batavia, New York, an historical museum, has a number of artifacts associated with Upton's career, including a sword, a sash, and other mementos. There is a statue of Upton in Batavia. The battlefields where Upton fought have changed somewhat in the last century, but the main outlines can still be followed. It is difficult to fully understand such engagements as Cold Harbor, Spotsylvania, or Rappahannock Station without a visit to the field itself. West Point, on the other hand, has changed little. Buildings have been added, but the spirit and organization remain as they were in 1860. The values of honor, manliness, excellence, discipline, and pride are still emphasized, as a visit to the academy makes clear.

Manuscripts

The largest block of Upton letters are in the Henry Algernon du Pont Papers, Winterthur Manuscripts, Eleutherian Mills Historical Library, Wilmington, Delaware. From about 1870 on Upton wrote to Du Pont frequently, especially during the periods they were working together on tactical reform. Further, many of Upton's other correspondents sent their letters from

Upton to Du Pont when they expected Du Pont to finish *The Military Policy of the United States*. The original manuscript of that book is also in the Du Pont Papers.

There are numerous Upton letters in various collections in the Manuscripts Division of the Library of Congress, including the William Conant Church Papers, the James A. Garfield Papers, the John Schofield Papers, the James Harrison Wilson Papers, and especially in the voluminous William T. Sherman Papers. The E. N. Gilpin Diary, also in the Library of Congress, was written by Upton's clerk during the Alabama-Georgia campaign of 1865 and contains much useful information. The F. V. Greene Papers, in the New York Public Library, New York City, and the Francis Lieber Correspondence, Henry Huntington Library, San Marino, California, contain Upton material.

Government Records

In the National Archives, Washington, D. C., is the "Appointment, Commission, and Personnel File of Emory Upton," a helpful source for recommendations, promotions, and appointments. The Superintendent's Letter Books in the archives of the United States Military Academy have material relating both to Upton's cadet career and his later service as Commandant. Upton's last will and testament is in the Genesee County Court House, Batavia, New York.

Government Publications

Any student of the United States Army feels a debt of gratitude to the government publication program. The volumes that have aided this study include, first of all, the various editions of Upton's own *Military Policy of the United States*, and the 128-volume set in which all serious investigation of a Civil War soldier must begin, *The War of the Rebellion; A Compilation of the Official Records of the Union and Confederate Armies*. Most of the publications from the Department of the Army contain helpful ideas and data. The basic work for any study of West Point in the fifties is the *Report of the Commission* (U. S. Senate, Miscellaneous Document No. 3, 36 Cong., 2 Sess., Washington, D. C., 1860). It contains historical material, statistical analysis, and a complete description of every course taught at the academy. Further, as a part of its research into the academy, the commission investigated every aspect of daily life, interviewed instructors and cadets, and visited classrooms. The result is a complete picture of West Point on the eve of the Civil War.

The Register of the Officers and Cadets of the U. S. Military Academy (West Point, New York), published annually from 1826, is an invaluable source for any study of either West Point or an individual cadet. The *Register* gives a list of the courses taken, the textbooks used, and the instructors for each class. It also contains the individual standings in each class for every cadet, as well as his general standing for the year.

The Centennial of the United States Military Academy at West Point (2 vols., Washington, D. C., 1904), is the most complete history of West Point, but it should be supplemented with George Washington Cullum, *Biographical Register of the Officers and Graduates of the U. S. M. A.* (3 vols., Boston 1891), and Sidney Forman, *West Point* (New York, 1950). R. Ernest Dupuy, *Where They Have Trod* (New York, 1940), contains some useful information.

Dates of appointment, promotion, service, and resignation of army officers can be found in the *Army Register*, published annually, or in Francis B. Heitman, *Historical Register and Dictionary of the U. S. Army, 1789–1903* (2 vols., Washington, D. C., 1903). Various Senate and House Reports are the most convenient place to find the arguments of Upton and his fellow reformers. Garfield, Burnside, and other Congressmen friendly to the army gave its officers a chance to make their views known in a series of hearings. The most important of these reports are *Army Organization* (U. S. House Report No. 33, 40 Cong., 3 Sess., Washington, 1869, *Army-Staff Organization* (U. S. House Report No. 74, 42 Cong., 3 Sess., Washington, 1873), and *Reorganization of the Army* (U. S. Senate Report No. 555, Pt. 2, 45 Cong., 3 Sess., 1879). Upton's influence on the World War I officer-corps can be traced in *Preparedness for National Defense: Hearings before the Committee on Military Affairs* (U. S. Senate Document, 64 Cong., 1 Sess., Washington, 1916).

Newspapers and Journals

An indispensable source for the post-Civil War army is the *Army and Navy Journal*. It is especially important for a study of Upton because of his friendship with the editor William C. Church. The *Journal*, which appeared weekly, contains information that cannot be found elsewhere. Second in importance only

to the *Journal* was the *United Service Magazine*. In the nineteenth
century the *Atlantic Monthly* and *The International Review*
occasionally carried articles on military reform; Upton contributed to all these journals. Newspapers used included the San
Francisco *Evening Bulletin* and the New York *Times*.

Biographies and Memoirs

Without the help of Peter S. Michie's *The Life and Letters of
Emory Upton* (New York, 1885), this study could not have been
undertaken. Michie, long time professor at the United States
Military Academy and friend of Upton, wrote a full and balanced
account of Upton's life. He made no attempt to analyze the
man or his influence, but he did include the pertinent events of
his career and printed letters not available elsewhere. Margaret
L. Coit's *John C. Calhoun: American Portrait* (Boston, 1950) and
the author's *Halleck: Lincoln's Chief of Staff* (Baton Rouge,
1960) contain information on pre-Civil War army reform. Otto
Eisenschiml's *The Celebrated Case of Fitz John Porter: An
American Dreyfus Affair* (New York, 1950), contains information
on the army in general and on Upton's participation in the
Porter trial. Both Liddell Hart's *Sherman* (New York, 1958) and
Lloyd Lewis' *Sherman: Fighting Prophet* (New York, 1932), are
excellent on Sherman's war career, but weak on his period as
General-in-chief. Philip C. Jessup's *Elihu Root* (2 vols., New
York, 1938) is a solid account of the man who relied so heavily
on Upton's writings for his ideas. Sheridan's, Sherman's, and
Grant's memoirs all have information on Upton, as does James
H. Wilson's *Under the Old Flag* (2 vols., New York, 1912).
John A Logan's *The Volunteer Soldier of America* (Chicago,
1887) is somewhat in the nature of a memoir and is an all-out
attack on Upton's ideas. Morris Schaff, *The Spirit of Old West
Point, 1858–1862* (Boston, 1907), has much on Upton's cadet
career. Theodore Clarke Smith, *The Life and Letters of James
A. Garfield* (2 vols., New Haven, 1925), is still the standard biog-
raphy. Benjamin P. Thomas and Harold M. Hyman, *Stanton*
(New York, 1962), is the best account of a nineteenth-century
Secretary of War, but the authors ignore most of the problems
Upton raised about both the position and Stanton himself. Donald
N. Bigelow's *William Conant Church and the Army and Navy
Journal* (New York, 1952) is a complete account of Upton's
friend.

Periodicals

Military Affairs, a scholarly journal published in Washington, D. C., has scores of articles that touch upon Upton or the post-Civil War army. Among the more helpful were Elbridge Colby's "Elihu Root and the National Guard," in Vol. XXIII (1959), John K. Mahon's "Civil War Infantry Assault Tactics," in Vol. XXV (1961), Frederick P. Todd's "Our National Guard: An Introduction to its History," in Vol. V (1941), an attack upon Upton, and Richard Brown's "General Emory Upton—The Army's Mahan," in Vol. XVII (1953), a brief but competent look at Upton.

The New York *Times Magazine* of June 16, 1918 has a provocative piece on "Emory Upton, Military Genius" by Richard Barry. Merritt Starr, "General Emory Upton—His Brothers, His Career," in the *Oberlin Alumni Magazine* for May, 1922, provides much family information. A typical attack on Upton is R. M. Cheseldine's "Where Upton Made His Big Mistake," in the *Infantry Journal*, March, 1930. An intelligent survey of American military though is Samuel P. Huntington's "Equilibrium and Disequilibrium in American Military Policy," *Political Science Quarterly* in Vol. LXXVI (1961). Huntington's insights are uncommonly good.

Tactical Studies

It is extremely difficult for anyone except a professional soldier to understand modern military tactics; it is close to impossible for anyone to comprehend nineteenth-century tactics. To begin with Upton's own *Infantry Tactics* (various editions, all published by D. Appleton and Company of New York) or the *Artillery Tactics* (New York, 1875) or *Cavalry Tactics* (1874) is to be illadvised—the student will almost surely get lost. Perhaps the best introduction is Robert S. Quimby, *The Background of Napoleonic Warfare: the Theory of Military Tactics in Eighteenth-Century France* (New York, 1957); then one must proceed to two older, but still good, works: A. F. Becke, *An Introduction to the History of Tactics, 1740–1905* (London, 1909), and Robert Greenhalgh Albion, *Introduction to Military History* (New York, 1929). Charles J. Ardant du Picq, *Battle Studies* (various translations) is a contemporary account by a soldier who shared many ideas with Upton. Finally, before proceeding to Upton's own works, consult Silas Casey's *Infantry Tactics* (3 vols., New York, 1862), and W. J Hardee, *Rifle and Light Infantry Tactics* (2 vols., Nashville, 1861).

General Works

The best way to start a study of any soldier is to make an effort to understand his professions and his traditions. Fortunately there are two eminently readable accounts filled with information and ideas: Theodore Ropp's *War in the Modern World* (paperback ed., New York, 1962) and Richard A. Preston, Sydney F. Wise, and Herman O. Werner, *Men in Arms: A History of Warfare and its Interrelationships with Western Society* (New York, 1956). Among other virtues, both are excellent on tactical developments and organizational change. For the American army, start with Walter Millis, *Arms and Men: A Study in American Military History* (New York, 1956) and T. Harry Williams, *Americans at War: The Development of the American Military System* (Baton Rouge, 1960) which are among the very few works that recognize the importance of the 1865–98 period and treat it intelligently. Slightly more specialized, but with more material on Upton, is Russell F. Weigley's *Towards an American Army: Military Thought from Washington to Marshall* (New York, 1962). No satisfactory history of the United States Army has been written; the best substitutes are C. Joseph Bernardo and Eugene H. Bacon, *American Military Policy: Its Development Since 1775* (2nd ed., Harrisburg, Penn., 1961) and William A. Ganoe, *The History of the United States Army* (New York, 1942). Still useful as an expression of pre-Civil War army thought is Henry W. Halleck, *Elements of Military Art and Science* (2nd ed., New York, 1862). All of John McAuley Palmer's works should be consulted for their forthright expression of the anti-Upton view in the army.

The basic work on the European soldier is Alfred Vagts, *A History of Militarism: Civilian and Military* (rev. ed., New York, 1959). Briefer, but with some sharp insights, is John W. Hackett, *The Profession of Arms* (London, 1962). Michael Howard, *The Franco-Prussian War* (New York, 1962), is a full treatment of the conflict that most influenced the soldiers of Upton's generation. Upton's own *The Armies of Asia and Europe* (New York, 1878) is still worth consulting, especially for organization of the armies. Jay Luvass, *The Military Legacy of the Civil War: The European Inheritance* (Chicago, 1959), shows that Europeans viewed the war in the same way Upton did.

On the development of the staff system, consult first of all Ropp, Williams, Millis, Vagts, and the Preston, Werner and Wise volume (all of which are helpful on any aspect of modern military history). The best account of the German experience is Gordon A. Craig, *The Politics of the Prussian Army, 1640-1945* (New York, 1956). Eugène Carrias, *L'Armée allemande. Son histoire, son organisation, son tactique* (Paris, 1938), is a full and balanced treatment; Walter Goerlitz, *History of the German General Staff, 1657–1945* (New York, 1953), is not as good as Craig. The spread of the staff idea can be traced in Spenser Wilkinson, *The Brain of an Army* (Westminster, England, 1895) and William H. Carter (who served under Upton), *Creation of the American General Staff,* U. S. Senate Document No. 119, 68 Cong., 1 Sess., Washington, 1924).

Upton's Civil War career can be followed in Isaac O. Best, *History of the 121st New York State Infantry* (Chicago, 1921), George T. Stevens, *Three Years in the Sixth Corps* (Albany, New York, 1866), Theodore F. Vaill, *History of the Second Connecticut Volunteer Heavy Infantry* (Winsted, Conn., 1868), and Bruce Catton, *A Stillness at Appomattox* (Garden City, New York, 1954). There are two good books on Oberlin: Robert S. Fletcher, *A History of Oberlin College* (2 vols., Oberlin, 1943), and James H. Fairchild, *Oberlin: The Colony and the College 1833–1883* (Oberlin, 1883).

Index

Printed in the USA.
CPSIA information can be obtained
at www.ICGtesting.com
LVHW010329170823
755467LV00001B/135